M Prior

THE

POETICAL WORKS

OF

MATTHEW PRIOR.

WITH A LIFE,

BY REV. JOHN MITFORD.

IN TWO VOLUMES.

VOLUME I.

BOSTON:
LITTLE, BROWN AND COMPANY.
NEW YORK: PHINNEY, BLAKEMAN AND MASON.
M.DCCC.LX.

RIVERSIDE, CAMBRIDGE:
STEREOTYPED AND PRINTED BY
H. O. HOUGHTON.

LINES TO —— ——

SENT WITH THIS VOLUME,

IN ALL OBEDIENCE, AS COMMANDED.

'Being your slave, what should I do but tend
 Upon the hours and times of your desire?
I have no precious time at all to spend,
 Nor services to do, till you require.'

SHAKSPEARE.

LOOK from thy flowery lattice ;—let me gaze
On that rich brow, that eye like morning bright,
That even sorrow wears a face of smiles
When thou art near ;—forth from thy lattice look,
My gentle —— ——— : and that golden day
Recall, when first by Deben's seaward shores,
Following the curving of his banks, we stray'd ;
Hand link'd in hand—sweet pilgrimage—and fill'd
With phantasies as sweet :—o'er ferny dell
We trode, and fields by reeking coulter torn,
And many a brook-fed mead, and islet green
With waving samphire—there the silver wave,
Obedient to the ocean's breath, just crept
To kiss the dewy margent :—so we pass'd

Pinnace, and barge, and fisher's skiff, whence flung
The thin net sway'd along, and to the shore
The boatman's carol sounded—farther now,
Following the inland waters, and our hearts
Surrendering to the genial influences
Of sun, and airs by soft Favonius breath'd;
Say, how we linger'd, pleasure gathering up
As children chase the insects o'er the plain,
From every sight and sound.—The bee's wild hum,
His wing in some rude foliature encag'd,
The beetle with its scaly habergeon
Fretting the margin of the pool—the path
Of the grey lizard to its sinuous home;
Or watch'd the seamew's silvery pennons shine
Above the sparkling waters; or far off
Following their flight,—the birds of nobler plume—
High-wing'd, and journeying to their distant home.

So on the river's crisped marge we stood,
Gazing the broad expanse, that like a lake
Lay folded in the mountain's soft embrace,
Fit haunt of nymph, or naiad.—Onward now
(What could we less, sweet nature's self our guide),
Up that dear path to vulgar eyes unseen,
With its grey shrine, and rural chapel crown'd,
Threading the oaken coppice, soon we gain'd
A little sylvan lawn, that 'mid the embrace
Of close-embowering trees, its tender green
Nurs'd with perennial dews:—the silent glade
To us, methought, was dedicate, and our's

It seem'd, alone its beauty :—to and fro,
The wild-rose shadows by the Summer's breath
Were moving ;—from the gnarled boughs above
The ring-dove pour'd its amorous plaint, and there
No more on man dependent, 'mid the leaves,
The red-breast built its Summer nest secure.

'Fit spot,' I cried, 'for Grecian bard to feign
Panisk, or fawn, amid the noonday heat
Reposing, or a band of paranymphs,
Such is the poet's high record, at eve
Discoursing in their soft Helladian tongue.
Or here, perchance, the silver-footed fays,
Tripping to moonlight minstrelsy, might start
The aged shepherd hastening down the glen.'—
Thou in this sylvan bower, 'mid tufted moss
And wrinkled fern, with colour'd weeds commix'd,
And glossy leaves of velvet texture, laid,
With hazel, and with hawthorn blossoms hung,
Like to a Tuscan lady in her bloom
Of richest beauty, as by Arno's vale,
Or where his shaded waters Arbia spreads,
Stepping from forth her princely halls, to taste
The breeze, entranc'd I've seen—thou, there re-clin'd;
Or as some gentle Dryad, who at eve
Just stealing from her timid covert, hears
Young Zephyr breathe his vow.—The day was clos'd;
The morning's roseate glow—The golden blaze
Meridian,—and the eve's purpureal sky.—

Oh day! as innocent, as fair!—and thou,
Fair as the day, and young and innocent,
Sweet maiden; thou not seldom to thine eye
(As oft again on these retiring sands
Thy evening footsteps shall be seen) wilt call
'Mid blushing smiles, and sunny tears, that speak
Of fond remembrance, all that memory holds
Of this sweet pilgrimage:—the winding shore,
The soft enamell'd margin—the long sweep
Of those majestic woods, which o'er the wave
Flung deep their emerald shadows,—the far hills;
The grey rock, with its blue springs trickling down
Through thick concealing foliage;—and the vale,
The long withdrawing vale, where Deben winds
His solitary wave from shore to shore,
To where the fountains of the Ocean lie.

J. M.

BENHALL,
20th September, 1835.

CONTENTS.

VOL. I.

LIFE OF MATTHEW PRIOR.

BY THE REV. JOHN MITFORD.

THERE appears to be great difficulty in settling, with correctness, the birth-place of Matthew Prior. In most of the biographies he is said to have been born in London; but in the register of his college, he is called at his admission, Matthew of Prior, Winburn, in Middlesex: on *the next day*, after his admission,[1] he himself signs his name, Matthew Prior, of Dorsetshire, in which county, as Dr. Johnson observes, and not in Middlesex, Winburn is found. When he stood candidate for a fellowship, five years afterwards, he was registered by himself, as of Middlesex. The last ought to be preferred, because it was made upon oath. He was born 21st July, 1664; in the college register he is styled Filius Georgii Prior generosi, a term that scarcely applies to the account of the Biogra-

1 Perhaps there is a slight mistake in reading the register, and it should stand—of Winburn AND Middlesex: at least, that would lessen the difference which now exists. Either the world Winburn is in toto a mistake, or the word *and* should be used for *in*: or the whole account must remain in its present contradictory state. If Prior's father was a joiner in London, it is not probable that he should belong to Winburn.

phia Britannica,[2] which describes his father as a citizen and joiner, being in good repute. Dr. Johnson thinks that he was willing to leave his birth unsettled: but it is to be observed, that the account which describes him of Winburn, and Parentis generosi, is written by the president of the college, and that one great mistake at the least, regarding the county in which his native place is found, exists in it. Yet the family appear to have had some land or property at Winburn, and to have parted with it; and so the term 'generosus' might apply to his father as a proprietor: it is, however, impossible to extricate the subject from difficulties that have too long closed round it to be removed.

At his father's death, which happened when he was young, he was affectionately received[3] into the house of his uncle, a butcher of respectability near Charing Cross, and by him placed under Dr. Busby at Westminster. There he remained sufficiently long to receive many of the advantages of a scholastic education, and he is said to have distinguished himself by his talents and acquirements. His uncle, however, removed him, after a certain time, with the intention of bringing him up to his own business. His house was in good repute, and

[2] See Biographia Britannica, p. 3438.

[3] Dr. Johnson says—He is supposed to have *fallen* into his uncle's hands,—a term not warranted by the earlier account of the Biographia. See also Prior's Life by Humphreys, prefixed to the 3rd vol. of his Poems, p. 1, 3rd ed.

frequented by some of the leading wits and patrons of the day, the Earl of Dorset among others.[4] It happened that the company differed with regard to the meaning of a passage in one of Horace's odes, when one of the gentlemen said—'I find that we are not likely to agree in our criticisms, but if I am not mistaken, there is a young fellow in the house, who is able to set us right.' Matthew Prior was immediately sent for, and explained the passage with such ability and modesty, as gained him the approbation of all present: and the Duke of Dorset from that time resolved to remove him from the tap of the Rummer to the more congenial bowers of the academy. He was accordingly sent to St. John's College, Cambridge, and in part supported by the generosity of his patron. 'Prior, says Burnet,[5] had been taken a boy out of a tavern by the Earl of Dorset, who accidentally found him reading Horace, and he, being very generous, gave him an education in literature.' He was admitted in 1682, in his eighteenth year, and taking his degree of Bachelor of Arts in 1686, was shortly after

4 S. Prior kept the Rummer tavern at Charing Cross, in 1685. The annual meeting of the nobility and gentry in the parish being held at his house, Oct. 14, 1685. See the lines

My uncle, rest his soul, when living,
Might have contrived the ways of thriving.

P. 3439, B. Brit.

5 See Burnet's History, vol. ii. p. 584.

chosen fellow of the college,[6] where, as Johnson observes, it may reasonably be supposed, that he was distinguished among his contemporaries. About two years after he wrote the poem on the Deity, which stands foremost in his volume. It was sent,[7] according to the established practice of the college, among others on sacred subjects, to the Earl of Exeter, in acknowledgment of a benefaction received from his ancestors : and Johnson thinks that it was well received, and that from Prior's mention of a picture, and of the countess's music, he was probably known to the family. It was during his residence at college, that he formed an intimacy with Charles Montagu, of Trinity College, afterwards the Earl of Halifax. In conjunction with him he wrote his well known travestie on Dryden's Hind and Panther, entitled—The Hind and Panther transversed to the story of the Country Mouse, and City Mouse, which was published in 1687.[8]

6 Dr. Johnson does not mention Prior's fellowship. His life of the poet is founded on that in the Biographia. This fellowship he retained to his death. When he was made ambassador, some one intimated that he ought to resign his fellowship; he answered "That every thing he had besides was precarious, and when all failed, that would be bread and cheese at the last, and therefore he did not mean to part from it."

7 Jacob says, 'a discerning eye might in this piece have seen the promises of a Solomon,' v. Lives of the Poets, vol. ii. p. 154. It was translated into Latin by Dobson, the translator of Milton's Paradise Lost.

8 'Did not Halifax,' asked Spence of Lord Peterborough, 'write the Country Mouse with Mr. Pryor?' Yes—just as

In the next year he wrote, as a college exercise, his ode on the necessary existence of the Deity. His abilities being now recognised, and becoming, as one of his biographers asserts, the delight and admiration of his contemporaries, he wisely endeavoured to advance his fortune by a wider acquaintance with the world. At the solicitation of his friend Fleetwood Shepherd,[9] he was introduced to the Earl of Dorset, and, in 1690, he was appointed secretary to the embassy that joined the Congress at the Hague: his conduct gave such satisfaction to his employers, that he was subsequently made gentleman of the bed-chamber to the king: and it is supposed that love and poetry equally occupied the leisure which he enjoyed. He wrote several small poems, and paid his addresses to Mrs. Elizabeth Singer, afterwards the famous Mrs. Rowe. In 1695 he joined with the general Corpus Poetarum by inditing an elegy on the death of Queen Mary, which Johnson suspects was never read by the afflicted monarch; but as he adds, that great part of the Musæ Anglicanæ was filled with poetic tears on the same subject; we may charitably excuse a king, who was never much given to poetry or lite-

if I was in a chaise with Mr. Cheselden here, drawn by his fine horse, and should say—Lord, how finely we draw this chaise.'

[9] See his Epistle to F. Shepherd, ending

My friend Charles Montagu's preferr'd,
Nor would I have it long observ'd,
That one man eats, while t'other's starv'd.

rature, and who was at that time more profitably employed in endeavouring to settle a general peace.[1]

Prior was again employed as secretary to the English negotiations at the treaty of Ryswick in 1697. Having been nominated the same year principal secretary of state in Ireland. In 1698 he was secretary to the embassy to France, in which he continued both under the Earl of Portland, and the Earl of Jersey: and where he was said to be considered of great distinction. An anecdote, honourable alike to his wit and his sincerity, is recorded in his memoirs:—Being shown the pictures at Versailles which Le Brun painted to commemorate the victories of Louis the XIVth, and being asked whether the King of England's Palace had any such decorations, he answered—'The monuments of my master's actions are to be seen everywhere but in his own house.'

He did not leave Paris till some time after the arrival of the Earl of Manchester, to whom his experience in foreign affairs, and his interest at the French Court, were of eminent service. In the middle of August, 1699, he went to King William in Loo in Holland, when, after a very particular audience with his majesty, he departed for England, and took possession of the under-secreta-

1 In the second volume of the Analecta Mus: Anglican: there is a copy of verses 'In obitum Augustissimæ et Desideratissimæ Reginæ Mariæ, by H. Sacheverell—G. Adams—Ant. Alsop—P. Foulkes—Ed. Chishull.

ry's seat, in the Earl of Jersey's office ; but he was soon ordered back to Paris to assist the ambassador. In the Christmas of this year, he printed his Carmen Seculare; in which King William received all the prodigality of a poet's commendation. Yet, as Johnson justly observes,—We must not accuse Prior of flattery. Of the domestic life, of the private virtues, and perhaps the temper of the monarch, no very favourable account could be given ; but his great public actions, his zeal in the cause of liberty and of Europe, his perseverance and inflexible steadfastness in adversity, his courage and military skill, acquit Prior of lavishing an inelegant and undistinguished praise : he said, that he praised others out of compliance with fashion, but that, in praising William, he followed his inclination.

In 1700, the university conferred on him the degree of master of arts : he succeeded Locke at the board of trade ; and he was elected representative of East Grinstead in Sussex, in 1701, when he seems to have changed his political opinions, and to have voted for impeaching the lords who were charged with advising the Partition treaty. He excuses himself, however, in one of his poems, (Conversation) by saying that he never approved the treaty, though obliged to carry it through in obedience to his sovereign.

Mathew, who knew the whole intrigue,
Nor much approved that mystic league.

During the reign of Anne, the negotiators and secretaries gave way to persons of more active virtues, and the sword took the place of the pen. Prior published his well known letter to Boileau on the Battle of Blenheim, and an ode addressed to the queen. Soon after he printed a volume of his poems, beginning with his College Exercise, and ending with his Nut-Brown Maid.[2] Eugène and Marlborough gave for some years ample employments to the court-poets, and accordingly, the Battle of Ramilies was celebrated by Prior, as Blenheim had been before. By some it has been believed, that the queen and the nation were wearied of the war, before the great commander who had so successfully prosecuted it, was inclined to listen to terms of pacification. It has been said, that Marlborough was influenced by private views in its continuance; perhaps, however, his sagacity and experience enabled him to foresee what still greater conquests his military talents, assisted by his powerful allies, could enable him to achieve: and he might not have been willing to have his long career of victories separated from the great end to which they were directed,—The reduction of the power of France, and the assured safety of the liberties of Europe. Prior joined the party of Harley in endeavouring to drive the whigs from power: and a paper called the Examiner was set

[2] On the origin of this poem of the Nut-Brown Maid, see Censura Literaria, vol. vi. p. 114.

up, of which much is said in Swift's works, and to which all the wits of the party contributed. One in ridicule of Garth's verses to Godolphin on the loss of his place was written by Prior, and answered by Addison. He is thought also to have been the author of a very satirical attack on the Duke of Marlborough, called the Widow and her Cat, which concludes with the following stanza:

> So glaring is thy insolence,
> So vile thy breach of trust is,
> That longer with thee to dispense
> Were want of power, or want of sense,
> Then, Towzer, do him justice.

The change in Prior's political sentiments did not pass unnoticed. He turned, says Pope, from a strong whig (which he had been when most with Lord Halifax) to a violent tory; and did not care to converse with any whigs after, any more than Rowe did with tories.

In 1711, Prior was appointed minister plenipotentiary to the Court of France, for the purpose of negotiating a peace. In a few weeks he returned, bringing with him Monsieur Mesnager, and the Abbé Gualtier. As the whole of this transaction was private, Prior and his companions were seized at Canterbury,[8] but immediately re-

[8] See account of Prior's arrest at *Deal*, in Scott's ed. of Swift, vol. ii. p. 356; and Annals of Queen Anne's Reign, p. 231, and vol. iv. p. 59.

leased by the queen's orders. The meetings were held at Prior's house, who was joined with the privy council in the commission to sign the articles, after the agreement; and who would have been joined with the two ministers at Utrecht, but the president, Lord Strafford, not willing to act with a person of so mean an extraction as Prior,[4] the business of trade was committed to the Lord Privy Seal; the letters of St. John and the queen, however, sufficiently evince their conviction of Prior's knowledge and services, especially in matters of trade. In 1712, he went to Paris, it is supposed with Lord Bolingbroke, to arrange those matters which remained unsettled at Utrecht. He had the appointments of an ambassador, though he did not assume the character till after the departure of the Duke of Shrewsbury. In October, he returned to England: bearing a private letter from the French King[5] to the queen, and returned in November. He remained at Paris in the character of a public minister for some

[4] Swift says, in his Journal to Stella,—'I dined with Lady Betty. I hear Prior's commission is passed to be ambassador extraordinary and plenipotentiary for the peace. ....And so I must go see his Excellency, 'tis a noble advancement, but they could do no less, after sending him to France. *Lord Strafford is as proud as hell*, and how he will bear one of Prior's mean birth on an equal character with him, I know not.'

[5] 'Prior was personally acceptable to Louis the XIVth, and well known to Boileau.' See Scott's Swift, iv. p. 75.

months after the accession of George the First, when he was succeeded by Lord Stair, who took possession of all his papers.[6] The proceedings of the new ministry against all who had any concern in the negotiations of the peace of Utrecht, were sufficient to put him on his guard, and made him expect the storm that soon followed. His letters to Bolingbroke, about this time, are full of anxiety and despondence. His private fortune was unsecured, he had nothing but the irregularly paid salary of his situation, and in his public capacity, he saw the long-gathered storm of a hostile party

6 'Prior had manifested much weakness at the time of Bolingbroke's attainder; his conduct was at least equivocal, if not treacherous; and it is said that it was the news, that he was returning from France, prepared to discover all he knew, and to save himself by the sacrifice of his friend, that prompted, or at least accelerated, Bolingbroke's sudden flight. Whether Prior really meant to implicate his patron admits, however, of much doubt. His evidence entirely disappointed the whigs, who had much relied on it, and they vented their wrath by the imprisonment of the poet for contempt and prevarication. We are not possessed of Bolingbroke's opinion of his conduct at this juncture, it probably caused a coolness between them, and there is no evidence that they ever again corresponded: but from the manner in which he mentions Prior's death, which happened before Bolingbroke's return to England, we may conclude that if he really considered his conduct to be treacherous, he felt rather pity than resentment for the traitor.' Cooke's Life of Bolingbroke, vol. ii. p. 19.

In one of his letters, Bolingbroke says,—'My friendship, dear Matt. shall never fail thee, employ it all, and continue to love Bolingbroke.' See Corr. vol. iii. p. 361.

ready to overwhelm him. On his arrival in England in March 1715, he was immediately taken up by an order of the council, and committed to the hands of a messenger. In April he underwent a short examination before the privy council, and at the conclusion was removed from his own house, to that of the messenger. Walpole made an impeachment against him, and he was ordered into close custody: and no person was admitted to see him without leave of the speaker. He was also, in 1717, excepted out of the act of grace; notwithstanding he was soon after discharged without any fresh prosecution or trouble. The arrears of his expenses, when allowed, had been procured for him by Lord Halifax, after great difficulty and delay. He wrote an account of the proceedings at his examination before the committee, which is to be found in his memoirs. His defence is left unfinished, and in what was done, he has not touched on one great objection, made particularly by Lord Bolingbroke and himself: that they were most *unseasonably witty* in the interludes of the most serious and important negotiations. The fact is, the orders received by the negotiators at Utrecht from the ministry in England respecting the conditions of the peace, and other articles dependent on it, do not appear to have been very clearly expounded. Lord Oxford's peace was wittily, though irreverently said, 'to be the peace of God—for it passed all human understanding.'[7] Prior mentions several difficulties on the articles of commerce which fell to his share.—'We had like, he said, to have made an Athanasian business of it at Utrecht, by that explanation of our own way of underrating our own commerce. Their letters to you are full of surmises and doubts that all was unhinged, and their letters to us again, that explanations, however made, were only to save appearances, and signified nothing. This melange, I say, and my endeavour to understand it, had like to make me run mad; if the Duke of Shrewsbury's good sense, and M. de Torcy's, not only good sense, but right understanding, had not redressed us!' In another place, Prior, who I believe was not a very skilful,

[7] At length great Anna said—'Let discord cease,'
She said, the world obey'd, and all was peace.

So sang Pope in his Windsor Forest:—his commentator, Dr. T. Warton, observes,—It may gratify a curious reader to see an extract of a letter of Prior to Lord Bolingbroke, written from Paris, May 18, 1713, concerning a medal that was to be struck on the Peace of Utrecht, so highly celebrated in this passage communicated to me by favour of the late Dutchess Dowager of Portland,—"I dislike your medal with the motto Compositis venerantur armis—I will have one of my own design; the queen's bust, surrounded with laurel, and with this motto, Annæ, Aug. felici Pacificæ, Peace in a triumphal car, and the words, Pax missa per orbem, this is ancient, this is simple, this is sense. Rosier shall execute it, in a manner not seen in England since Simon's time."—See Warton's Pope, vol. i. p. 133.

or successful negotiator, calls it,—The d—d peace of Utrecht.

With the fall of the tory ministry, a fall as much owing to their own selfish intrigues and unprincipled designs, as to the power of the whigs, Prior's connection with public life and political cares was terminated. It is apparent, from his correspondence, that he had for some time foreseen his fall, though he had no power of providing against its consequences. He left his diplomatic honours as poor as when he first assumed them. He spent the remainder of his days at a small villa, called Down Hall, in Essex, which his old patron Lord Oxford gave him for his life. His chief pecuniary resources were drawn from his Fellowship.[8] Having finished his Solomon[9] on the Vanity of the World, he collected a volume of his poems, and dedicated them to the Duke of Dorset, as a memento of his former patronage. The price of the volumes was two guineas, and the whole

[8] 'Prior hates his commission of the Customs because it spoils his wit. He says, he dreams of nothing but cockets and dockets, and drawbacks, and other jargon, words of the Custom House.'—Swift to Stella.

[9] 'Our friend Prior, not having had the vicissitude of human things before his eyes, is likely to end his days in as forlorn a state as any other poet has done before him, if his friends do not take more care of him, than he did of himself. Therefore, to prevent the evil, which we see is coming on very fast, we have a project of printing his *Solomon*, and other poetical works by subscription, one guinea

collection produced four thousand. Soon after he formed a very judicious design of writing a history of his own time; which, doubtless, would have contained some valuable and authentic materials, as he was a near spectator, as well as active agent in all the most important political occurrences, till the dissolution of the tory ministry. A lingering fever, however, put a period to his existence, Sept. 18, 1721, in the 58th year of his age. He died at Wimple, near Cambridge, the seat of Lord Oxford at the time, but which was subsequently purchased by the Hardwicks. He was buried, at his own desire, in Westminster Abbey, and five hundred pounds were set apart by him in his will, to erect a monument to his memory. The bust was executed by Coriveaux, and the Latin inscription, which is much too long, written by Freind.[10] Prior appears to have had a *tendresse* towards a lady called Mrs. Elizabeth Cox, whom he left residuary legatee in his will: and who is

to be paid in hand, and the other at the delivery of the book. He, Arbuthnot, Pope, and Gay are with me and remember you. It is our joint bequest that you will endeavour to procure some subscriptions. You will give your receipts for the money you receive, and when you return it hither, you shall have others in lieu. There are no papers printed here, nor any advertisement to be published; for the whole matter is to be managed by friends, in such a manner as shall be least shocking to the dignity of a plenipotentiary.' Letter from Erasmus Lewis to Swift, v. Swift's works, vol. xi. p. 460, ed. Nichols.

[10] See Appendix No. I.

described as humoursome and imperious: this, however, poets, and other than poets have borne before and since the days of Prior: but Mrs. Cox was without any share of that beauty, which, in the eye of a man of imagination and taste, is a 'pearl of great price,' and which at least is some compensation for the inconveniences of female caprice. Against ill temper, and ill looks combined, I know nothing but a resignation to fate, and a conviction that misery has no other arrows so cruel, and so malignant in store. Prior left his college a set of books of the value of £200, to be chosen out of his library, and his own picture by La Belle, together with that of Lord Jersey. The books are said to be in very superb bindings, and the portrait represents him as an ambassador, very richly dressed. It was said to be a present to Prior from Louis XIV. and cost a hundred pistoles.

Prior, I am afraid, was not a more able negotiator than the ministers who employed him; but he was a warm partisan, and privately as well as politically attached to the Earl of Oxford. Many of his letters are to be found in the Bolingbroke correspondence, but 'Prior,' says Mr. Coxe,[1] 'made

1 See Coxe's Life of Sir R. Walpole, vol. i. p. 761, who adds,—'His friend Steele was wholly incapable of application, and Addison was a miserable secretary of state.' Pope says,—Prior was nothing out of verse, and was less fit for business than even Addison, though he prized him-

but an indifferent negotiator.' His contemporaries have supplied us with little information as to the lighter parts of his life. His deportment seemed to be gay, and his conversation humourous and pleasant. One of his answers to a vain coxcomb of a Frenchman is worth reporting. Prior was at the opera seated next to a person who accompanied with his voice the principal singer; Prior began abusing the performer in the strongest terms of reproach, till the Frenchman expostulated with him for censuring a person of acknowledged merit. 'I

self much upon his talents for it. What a simple thing was it to say upon his tombstone, that he was writing a history of his own times! he could not write in a style fit for history, and I dare say he never had set down a word toward any such thing. Swift, however, calls Mr. Prior a person of great distinction, not only on account of his wit, but for his abilities in the management of affairs. See Last Years of Q. Anne, p. 78, ed. Nichols. See Cooke's Life of Bolingbroke, vol. i. p. 165. In a letter from Ld. Bolingbroke to Q. Anne, Sept. 20, 1711, he writes, 'My Lord Treasurer moved, and all my Lords were of the same opinion, that Mr. Prior should be added to those who are empowered to sign. The reason for which is, because he having personally treated with Mons. de Torcy, is the best witness we can produce of the sense in which the general preliminary engagements are entered into. Besides which, *as he is the best versed in matters of trade* of all your majesty's servants, who have been trusted in this secret, if you shall think fit to employ him in the future treaty of commerce, it will be of consequence that he has been a party concerned in concluding that convention, which must be the rule of this treaty.' In one of his letters to Ld. Bolingbroke, he signs himself—M. Prior, animal peregrine missum ad mentiendum R. P. causâ.

know all that, said Prior, mais il chante si haut, que je ne sçaurois vous entendre.' In a French company, when every one sang a little song or stanzas, of which the burden was given,— Banissons la Mélancolie,— when it came to his turn to sing, after the performance of a young lady, he produced these extemporary and elegant lines:

Mais cette voix, et ces beaux yeux
Font Cupidon trop dangereux,
Et je suis triste quand je crie
Banissons la mélancolie.

Prior never had much money at command, and either by reason that he had not wherewithal to purchase the venal favours of the higher class of beauties, perhaps from indolence, or perhaps from a naturally inferior taste, he is said to have been coarse and low in his amours. Prior, says Pope, was not a right good man. He used to bury himself for whole days and nights together with a poor mean creature, and often drank hard. He left most of his effects to the poor woman he kept company with — his Chloe. Every body knows what a wretch she was; I think she had been a little alehouse keeper's wife, and Spence adds, 'that after the death of her friend the Poet, she became the wife of a country cobbler.' Arbuthnot wrote to Mr. Watkins —" Prior had a narrow escape by dying, for if he had lived he had married a brimstone bitch, one Bessy Cox, that keeps an alehouse in Long Acre. Her husband died about a month ago, and Prior has left his estate between his servant

Jonathan Drift,[1] and Bessy Cox. Lewis got drunk with punch with Bess night before last. Do not you say where you had this news of Prior. I hope all my mistress' (Q. Anne's) ministers will not behave themselves so. We are to have a bowl of punch at Bessy Cox's. She would fain have put it upon Lewis that she was his (Prior's) Emma. She owned *Flanders Jane* was his Chloe. I know of no security against this dotage in batchelors, but to repent of their misspent time, and marry with speed."—The Duchess Dowager of Portland (says Hannah More) was Prior's noble, lively little Peggy. Dr. Johnson calls his Chloes dirty drabs and despicable, who stole his plate and ran away. Richardson says, Prior would leave Pope and Swift, and smoke his pipe with a common soldier and his wife in Long Acre. Yet, if we believe Swift, Prior was much loved and esteemed both by Bolingbroke and Harley, as he well deserved, upon account of every virtue that can qualify a man for private conversation. In another place he commends his talent as a punster. Mr. Hazlitt says 'Some of Prior's bon mots are the best that are recorded.' Johnson, however, considers that his opinions were correct and right, though his life was loose and sensual: a distinction rather dangerous for a moralist to maintain, unless he believes our reason to be unaffected by our passions and our will: and that the integrity of the mind can long coexist with

[1] V. p. xxi. '*Adrian* Drift, his executor.'

the degradation of the appetites, the impurity of the affections, and the seductive wanderings of the heart. From such anecdotes as the above, as well as from his works, we should judge our poet to have been a person of an easy, indolent, and careless turn of mind ; who having passed through the business of his early life, and acquired an independence of fortune by the kindness of his friends, spent the remainder of his days in a leisure, where amusement could be acquired with the least trouble, and with indifference towards all who censured the indelicacy of his choice, and the coarseness of his company. In one of Bolingbroke's letters to Sir Thomas Hanmer, he writes—If I have the honour of a line from you, pray give me some account of Mat's private life. Once I was in the gentleman's secret, but his last despatch contains, in almost a ream of paper, nothing but solemn accounts of baseness, such as made me expect to find Jo. Werden instead of Mat. Prior at the bottom of the voluminous epistle. We hear much of a *certain eloped nun*[1] *who has supplanted the nut-brown maid.*

Many years after Prior's death there appeared a small volume called—The History of his own time, compiled from the original manuscripts[2] of

[1] This person is alluded to in a subsequent letter of Prior, as his *réligieuse défroquée.*

[2] The title-page has this motto underneath—"I had rather be thought a good Englishman, than the best poet, or greatest scholar, that ever wrote." Matt. Prior.

his late Excellency Matthew Prior, Esq. It was copied for the press by Mr. Adrian Drift, his executor, and is dedicated to Lord Oxford. After his death, they came into possession of Charles Foreman, Esq. who had intended to publish them; but dying before his design was executed, the papers were delivered to Mr. Bancks. As the author of the article on Prior's life in the Biographia Britannica observes, "Notwithstanding all this parade, upon the perusal, very little of Mr. Prior's writing will be found in this piece." Of Prior's personal appearence I am not aware that any description has been given. Swift, in his Journal to Stella, incidentally mentions, that he walked to make himself fat, and that he generally had a cough; [3] and Lord Bolingbroke, in a letter to M. de Torcy, writes —"Au surplus, vous voulez bien que je me remette à ce que j'aurai l'honneur de vous écrire en deux jours d'ici par son Excellence Matthieu. Je crois que vous le trouverez instruit à finir toutes les choses, *et que malgré sa phisionomie, qui n'est pas des plus heureuses*, il ne sera pas perdu pour le coup;" and in a subsequent one, speaking also of *Matthieu*, he says '*Ce visage de bois* ne commencera son voyage que Lundi prochain;' and his cor-

[3] "The days are now long enough to walk in the park after dinner, and so I do whenever it is fair. This walking is a strange remedy. Mr. Prior walks to make himself fat, and I to bring myself down. He has generally a cough, which he only calls a cold. We often walk round the park together." Journ. to Stella, b. xiv. 361.

respondent, in one of his answers, observes "Vous vous avez renvoyé, my lord, sous *l'extérieur* de Matthieu, le véritable fils de Mons. Bays: il ne lui manque que de remplir la verre de son père. Il est d'ailleurs aussi Hollandois, et je crois beaucoup plus opiniâtre." But we must now turn to his poetry.

Dr. Johnson[4] has observed, that Prior's works may be considered *distinctly* as comprising Tales, Love verses, occasional Poems, the Alma, and the Solomon. Taking then this distribution, we may observe, that in his *Tales*, he has caught the quaint humour and comic power of Fontaine, the sly archness, the freedom of expression, and the natural graces of composition. Some grossness, indeed, which belonged to the original, and which were the dregs of a former age, and not rejected by the levity of his, still remain;[5] the books from which both Prior and the French poet borrowed their droll and humorous narrations were seldom free from a licentiousness that was used as a founda-

[4] On Johnson's criticism on Prior, see Cowper's Letters, vol. i. p. 318, second series, 8vo.

[5] Of Hans Carvel, Goldsmith says —'This bagatelle, for which, by the bye, Prior has got his greatest reputation, was a tale told in all the old Italian collection of jests, and borrowed from thence by Fontaine. It had been translated once or twice before in English, yet was never regarded till it fell into the hands of Mr. Prior. A strong instance how much every thing is improved in the hands of a man of genius.' See B. of Engl. Poetry, ii. 58.

tion for wit. It would, however, be difficult to say how such stories could be more gracefully or agreeably told.

Dr. Johnson thinks that Prior is less happy in his amorous effusions; and he compares them to Cowley's artificial sorrows. But in the first place, there is an ease and simple elegance in them which Cowley seldom possesses: in some there is a softness and tenderness of complaint conveyed with the utmost felicity of expression; and for the classical and mythological allusions, they are gaily and sportingly inserted; introduced with some happy allusion, and accompanied by some agreeable and unexpected turn. To shut out all allusions to the beautiful fictions of ancient mythology, would be to rob poetry of one of its richest provinces, a province created by the finest genius, and embellished by the most captivating fancy.

The serious odes of Prior are totally wanting in lyrical power. Without possessing the strict orderly arrangement which belongs to the model and form of lyric poetry, they are also devoid of the fire, the abruptness, the bold transitions, the change of numbers, the figures, which the ode demands: Prior uses the word ode in a very unusual and unrestricted sense. His ode to Col. G. Villiers is an elegy, and written in the common heroic lines; one merit it possesses in having furnished Pope with the conclusion of his Epistle from Heloisa to Abelard.[6] His Epistle to Boileau is sprightly and elegant; and his burlesque on the same poet's ode on Namur, is executed with infinite wit and taste. Of Prior's epigrams it is sufficient praise to say that they are among the best which we possess, and are found in every collection: for many of them he is believed to be indebted to the French: Dr. Johnson discovered the Thief and Cordelier in the almost forgotten poems of George Sabinus. The translation of Callimachus is stiff and hard; indeed the severe and highly wrought style of the original was unsuited to Prior's lighter pen. In his ode in the manner of Spenser, he has totally destroyed the beautiful system of versification in which the bard of Mulla enshrined his Fairy Queen; and adopted, by way of improvement, one consisting of two quatrains, and ending with an heroic verse and an alexandrine, a poor and wretched

6 Prior's ode on the Queen's death may be traced in Collins's Ode to Thompson: and a feather from his poem 'the Dove,' has dropped into Gray's long story. From Prior, says Mr. Southey, Pope adopted some of the most conspicuous artifices of his verse. V. Spec. of Engl. Poets, i. p. xxx. Malone supposes that Prior may have written the epitaph on Cecil, fifth Earl of Exeter. See it in Scott's Dryden, vol. xv. 191. The Judgment of Venus, in Prior's works, is said to be written by Mr. Harcourt. See Dunster's ed. of Philips' Cyder, p. 96. See some poems supposed to be by Prior in Nichols' Select Poems, vol. iv. p. 46-55, also a Latin poem on the marriage of George, Prince of Denmark, and the Lady Anne, vol. vii. p. 93.

substitute for the linked sweetness, and the finely suspended harmony of the original. Prior's well known tale of Henry and Emma[7] appears to me much inferior to the original ballad, as it wants its freshness and simplicity. The subject is drawn out in continued accusation, and concession, to a length that fatigues. The tenderness and feeling are smothered in a cloud of words, lost in general reflections and maxims of morality, and destroyed

7 On the original ballad of Henry and Emma, see Censura Literaria, vol. vi. p. 114. It is but fair to say, that Cowper's authority as regards this poem is against the editor, and therefore it is given in this note. 'But what shall we say of his rusty-fusty remarks upon Henry and Emma? I agree with him, that morally considered, both the knight and his lady were bad characters, and that each exhibits an example which ought not to be followed. The man dissembles in a way that would have justified the woman had she renounced him, and the woman resolves to follow him at the expense of delicacy, propriety, and even modesty itself. But when the critic calls it a dull dialogue, who will believe him? There are few readers of poetry of either sex in this country who cannot remember how that enchanting piece has bewitched them, who do not know, that instead of finding it tedious, they have been so delighted with the romantic turn of it, as to have overlooked all its defects, and to have given it a consecrated place in their memories, without ever feeling it a burthen.' See letter, Jan. 17, 1782. As regards Dr. Johnson's criticisms on Prior, there is much that is correct, and much not exactly to the purpose. It is clear that he preferred without labour, drawing on his general stores of criticism for remark, to reading Prior with diligence and exactness. His Lives of the Poets always show his vigour of intellect, sometimes the imperfection of his knowledge, sometimes his prejudice, and too often his indolence.

by the fanciful and ingenious images which are brought to illustrate them. The whole is too much in the style of the Pastor fido, and the Italian pastorals. The utmost praise must be given to the elegance of the diction, and the easy and varied flow of the numbers: but the whole piece is too artificial and elaborate. It seems rather a combat of skill and ingenuity, a desire to torment and to perplex, than a trial of anxious and mistrusting love: and perhaps, after all, the impression from the moral is not satisfactory. The repeated and increasing sacrifices which the lover demands, would hardly be compatible with that female dignity and fine sense of honour, which is built on a proud consciousness of innocence, and without which love cannot be supported.

Of the poem of *Solomon*,[8] the general opinion seems to be correct. It may indeed be studied by the poetical artist, for the flow and harmony of its polished versification, and its beautifully selected and finished language;[9] but it is too long, too uniform, and too serious and majestic. The weighty

[8] Cowper considers 'the *Solomon* to be the best poem, whether we consider the subjects of it, or the execution, that he ever wrote.' V. Letters to Unwin, Jan. 5, 1782.

[9] There is one piece of absurdity in the second book of Solomon, which one would have thought the taste of Prior would have rejected. *Abra* is going to give a dinner to Solo mon.

Abra invites—the nation is the guest:
To have the honour of each day sustain'd,

and massive wisdom, the axiomatic and pregnant brevity of the original are diffused into a flowing eloquence and weakened by ornamental diction. The current of the story moves languidly along: and wants that variety of embellishment, and that force of illustration, which draws its examples from the history of men and of society, and which Pope so happily introduces into the Essay on Man—

To point a moral, or adorn a tale.

Of the *Alma*,[1] the only defects appear to be in

The woods are traversed, and the lakes are drain'd;
Arabia's wilds, and Egypt's are explored,
The *edible creation* decks the board,
Hardly the Phœnix scapes!!

[1] Mr. Pope said that the Alma of Prior was the only work that, abating its excessive scepticism, he could wish to have been the author of. Yet so unable, said he, are authors to make a true estimate of what they write, either from the fondness of their subject, or the pains it costs them in the composition, that Prior, asking him soon after the publication of his works by subscription how he liked his *Solomon*, he replied,—Your *Alma* is a masterpiece. The other, with great impatience and resentment, replied,—" What, do you tell me of my *Alma*, a loose and hasty scribble to relieve the tedious hours of imprisonment, while in the messenger's hand."—This judgment of his friend occasioned these two satiric lines in the small poem of the *Impertinent*. (The Conversation.)

Indeed, poor Solomon in rhyme
Was much too grave to be sublime.

See Ruffhead's Life of Pope, 8vo. p. 482. Goldsmith

its rambling and inconclusive plan. Though formed (it is said) upon the model of Hudibras, there is sufficient originality to redeem it from the servility of a copy. Inferior in its pregnant brevity of wit, and unexpected quaintness of allusion, but far excelling in easy and graceful turns of thought: and in the unaffected clearness of its language, which flows on with perfect ease, as if totally unembarrassed by the restraints of rhyme. Of Prior's larger poems it is undoubtedly the most perfect.

To Prior must be allotted the praise of giving a grace and delicacy of finish to our versification, which alone was wanting among the improvements introduced by Dryden; and in which he was scarcely inferior to Pope. In this respect, compared to Prior, Denham and Waller,[1] appear rugged and unfinished. To this refinement, Prior was

says, (see his Beauties of Eng. Poetry, vol. ii. p. 205,) "What Prior meant by this poem I can't understand. By The Greek motto to it, one would think it was either to laugh at the subject or his reader. There are some parts of it very fine, and let them save the badness of the rest." Shenstone observed, that Pope never mentions Prior, though so handsomely spoken of in the Alma. One might imagine that Mr. Pope, *indebted as he was to Prior* for such numberless beauties, should have readily repaid this poetical obligation. This can only be imputed to pride, or party cunning; but Prior's name twice occurs in the Dunciad, B. ii. C. 124, 138, though but slightly.

[1] Our poetry was not quite harmonized in Waller's time: so that this which would be now *looked upon as a slovenly sort of versification*, was, with respect to the time in which it was

probably led by his familiarity with the French poets, and by his choice, like them, of those light and *miniature* subjects, which derive half their merit from minuteness of finish, and delicacy of touch. It would appear, at first sight, that he was more defective in the accuracy of his rhymes,[2] than might have been supposed: but a very great latitude had been allowed in that respect, till Pope's example, stimulated by Swift's fastidiousness, corrected the evil: the few hemistichs which he introduces in his Solomon, were probably intended to relieve the monotony of the piece: Prior perhaps cannot be called a *great* poet:[3] but he has the merit of writing in a style and manner formed with such taste and skill,[4] with such knowledge of the laws of poetry, and such attention to the choice of

written, almost a prodigy of harmony.—Goldsmith, B. Engl. Poetry, ii. 91.

2 The chief are—has, face—means, intends—carvel, barrell—relief, life—frowns, surrounds—voice, noise—kindness, fineness—lawn, man—proclaim, swain—such rhymes as *way* and *sea* were allowed. Pope always rhymes *tea* to such words: it was then pronounced as in French.

3 See verses by Prior to lady Henrietta Harley, not in the common edition of his works in Scott's ed. of Swift, vol. xvi. p. 328.

4 Pope mentions Prior in the list which he drew up of writers who might serve as authorities for poetical language; it was begun twice, but left imperfect. There were but nine mentioned, and two of these only in the burlesque style.—Spenser Shakspeare, Fletcher, Waller, Butler, Dryden, *Prior*, Swift.—V. Spence's Anecdotes, p. 311.

words, and beauty of language, as to prove that he was a great proficient in his art. In his own lively, picturesque, and gay manner, he is still unrivalled, and he may justly be called the first poet, of the *dressed* age of poetry, and who brought to perfection the polished ease, the vivacity and graces of the French school.

APPENDIX.

I.

Sui temporis Historiam meditante
Paulatim obrepens Febris
Operi simul et vitæ filum abripuit.
Sep. 18. An. Dom. 1721. ætat. 57.
H. S. E.
Vir eximius
Serenissimis
Regi Gulielmo, Reginæque Mariæ
In congressione fœderatorum
Hagæ Anno 1690 celebrata
Deinde Magnæ Britanniæ Legatis
Tum iis
Qui Anno 1697 Pacem Ryswicki confecerunt
Tum iis
Qui apud Gallos Annis proximis Legationem obierunt
Eodem etiam Anno 1697 in Hibernia
Secretarius
Necnon in utroque honorabili confessu
Eorum
Qui Anno 1700 ordinandis commercii negotiis
Quique Anno 1711 dirigendis Portorii rebus
Præsidebant
Commissionarius
Postremo
Ab Anna
Felicissimæ Memoriæ Reginâ
Ad Ludovicum XIV. Galliæ Regem
Missus Anno 1711
De Pace stabilienda

(Pace etiamnum durante
Diuque ut boni jam omnes sperant duratura)
Cum summa potestate Legatus
Matthæus Prior Armiger
Qui
Hos omnes, quibus cumulatus est, titulos
Humanitatis, ingenii, eruditionis laude
Superavit
Cui enim nascenti faciles arriserunt musæ
Hunc Puerum Schola hic regia perpolivit.
Juvenem in collegio S'ti Johannis
Cantabrigia Optimis scientiis instruxit
Virum denique auxit, et perfecit
Multa cum viris Principibus consuetudo
Ita natus, ita institutus,
A vatum choro, avelli nunquam potuit
Sed solebat sæpe rerum Civilium gravitatem,
Amæniorum literarum studiis condire
Et cum omne adeo Poetices genus
Haud infeliciter tentaret
Tum in fabellis concinne lepideque texendis
Mirus Artifex
Neminem habuit parem
Hæc liberalis animi oblectamenta
Quam nullo illi labore constiterint
Facile ii perspexere, quibus usus est Amici
Apud quos Urbanitatem et leporum plenus
Cum ad rem quæcunque forte inciderat
Aptè, variè copiosèque alluderet
Interea nihil quæsitum, nihil vi expressum
Videbatur
Sed omnia ultro effluere
Et quasi jugi e fonte affatim exuberare
Ita suos tandem dubios reliquit
Essetne in Scriptis Poeta eleqantior
An in Convictu, Comes jucundior.

II. *Extract from Warton's Pope on the MSS. of Prior.*

'Our friend Dan Prior told, you know,
A tale extremely à propos.'

I HAVE frequently wondered how sparing Pope has been in general in his praises of *Prior*, especially as the latter was the intimate friend of Swift and Lord Oxford. I imagine this reserve is owing principally to some satirical epigrams that Prior wrote on Atterbury. The Alma is not the only composition of Prior, in which he has displayed a knowledge of the world, and of human nature: for I was once permitted to read a curious manuscript, late in the hands of her Grace the Duchess Dowager of Portland, containing essays and dialogues of the dead, on the following subjects by Prior:

1. Heads for a Treatise on Learning.
2. Essay on Opinion.
3. A Dialogue between Charles the Fifth and Herard the Grammarian.
4. Betwixt Locke and Montayne.
5. The Vicar of Bray and Sir Thomas More.
6. Oliver Cromwell and his Porter.[1]

[1] See Spence's Anecdotes, p. 48. Prior kept every thing by him, even to all his school exercises. There is a manuscript collection of this kind, in his servant Drift's hands, which contains at least half as much as all his published works. And there are nine or ten copies of verses among them, which I thought much better than several things he himself published. In particular, I remember there was a dialogue of about two hundred verses, between Apollo and Daphne, which pleased me as much as any thing of his I ever read. There are also four dialogues in prose, between persons of characters very strongly opposed to one another,

If these pieces were published, Prior would appear to be as good a prose writer, as a poet. It seems to be growing a little fashionable to decry his great merits as a poet. They who do this, seem not sufficiently to have attended to his admirable ode to Mr. Charles Montagu, Earl of Halifax. His ode to the queen, 1706, and his epistle and ode to Boileau: most of his tales, the Alma here mentioned; the Henry and Emma, (in which surely are many strokes of tenderness and pathos) and his Solomon, a poem which, however faulty in its plan, has yet very many noble and finished passages, and which has been so elegantly and classically translated by Dobson, as to reflect honour on the College of Winchester, where he was educated, and where he translated the first book as a school exercise. I once heard him lament, that he had not at that time read Lucretius, which would have given a richness, and variety, and force to his verses, the only fault of which seems to be a monotony, and want of different pauses, occasioned by translating a poem in rhyme, which he avoided in his Milton. It is one mark of a poem intrinsically good that it is capable of being well translated. The political conduct of Prior was blamed on account of the part he took in the famous partition treaty; but in some valuable memoirs of his life, written by the honourable Mr. Montagu, his friend, which were also in the possession of the Duchess Dowager of Portland, this conduct is clearly accounted for, and amply defended. In those memoirs are many curious and interesting particulars of the history of that time.

which I thought very good. One of them was between Charles the Fifth and his tutor Adrian. The sixth, to show the different turns of a person who had studied human nature, only in his closet, and of one who had rambled all over Europe. Another, between Montayne and Locke, on a most regular and a very loose way of thinking. A third, between O. Cromwell and his mad Porter, and the fourth, between Sir Thomas More and the Vicar of Bray. (Pope.)

In a curious and original letter which I have read, by the favour of the late Duchess Dowager of Portland, Prior speaks thus slightingly of the *veracity* of the celebrated Earl of Peterborough to Lord Oxford, Feb. 10, 1714.—"Lord Peterborough, says he, is gone from Genoa in an open boat—that's *one*; 300 miles by sea—that's *two*; that he was forced ashore twenty times by tempests and majorkeens, to lie among the rocks—that's—*how many*, my lord treasurer?"

III. *From Bolingbroke's Correspondence.* 4 vols. 8vo.

Sept. 1712. * * * What I trouble you with is, you see, a parcel of letters, which have been brought hither, and where left during my writing from Fontainbleau. They are, I believe, of no great worth, and might have staid on this side for ever. Indeed, they had like to have done so, for your friend Matt has for fifty hours past had a *trousse-galante dans toutes les formes*, and I was of opinion that I was going *ad Palamedem, ad Ulyssem, et Heroas.* I have changed this opinion these twelve hours past, and I hope to live with Lord Treasurer and Lord Bolingbroke, who are e'en as good company; why do I not hear from you all?

Jan. 1713—Matt to Henry.—I have heard no more from the Congress at Utrecht, than if it were the council of Jerusalem. What last I had from you thence, I faithfully transferred to you, expecting your orders thereupon. If you agree with the proposal of Newfoundland, which is the same you and I (N. B. this is Matt and Harry) laid down: and if we can take 1664 for our plan, in order to reduce the traffic to that era, the peace is made. Otherwise I see no shore. Not but that I am ready to swim as long as you please *in alto mari or super altum mare*, for that you will remember was a point of grammar long discussed: as are some other points, arrogat, or assumpsit, and—parlons d'autres choses. * * * * I have made your compliments to my Lady Duchess, and thank you for the hint as to the morbré in truffles.[1] 'Non sunt contemnenda quasi parva, sine quibus magna constare non possunt.'

April 8, 1713. * * *

TO HIS GRACE THE DUKE OF SHREWSBURY.

(With Montaign's Essays inclosed in the above Letter.)

DICTATE, oh, mighty judge, what thou hast seen
Of cities and of courts, of books and men,
And deign to let thy servant hold thy pen.

Through ages thus I might presume to live,
And from the transcript of thy prose receive
What my own short-liv'd verse can never give.

Thus should fair Britain, with a gracious smile,
Receive the work ; the venerable isle,
For more than treaties made, should bless my toil.

Nor longer hence the Gallic style preferr'd,
Wisdom in English idiom should be heard,
While Shrewsbury told the world when Montagne err'd.

—Are they good ? What think you of an oak, which is Britain ; a trophy of arms at the bottom of it, a wreath of palm hung on the tree ; over the trophy, innumeris potior.

[1] This passage alludes to some trifles which he had sent to Q. Anne.

1713, May 10. * * Brother Sim is here, very well and hearty. He tells me, you have rescued Cato from Whigism. I have spoke to Lord Chamberlain concerning Booth, and I believe we may procure any encouragement for him that is reasonable. Note, *Cato* means Addison, who, though by party a Whig, associated with the principal men on the Tory side. The day on which the account of the peace arrived, he dined with Bolingbroke.

1713, Sept.—Poor Dick Skelton dines sometimes, I think, in York Buildings. He has done so these three years, but colic, spleen, and disappointment, sour people's digestion. Pray persist in your good opinion of him, my Lord, for he really deserves it from you. I have likewise engaged the Duke of Shrewsbury to put in a kind word in his behalf; for what, in God's name, do we translate our odes, and write our little stuff, but to be able to do our friends some good? And why is a man, who may be useful to the public, and whose heart is with us, to lie fallow till either we have not the power to do him service, or till he wants health to enjoy our friendly offices? I wish I had a word from Lord Treasurer; but wishes are vain, and sighs cannot obtain, as Sir Car Seroop most elegantly expresses it. * * *

1713. * * Adieu, my dear Lord; if at my return I may help you any way in your drudgery, the youngest clerk you have is not more at your command: and if at the old hour of midnight after your drudgery, a cold bladebone of mutton in Duke Street will go down sicut olim, it, with all that belongs to the master of the house (except Nanny) is entirely yours. Adieu. May God bless you, men respect you, and women love you.

1714, Jan, 18.—The very apprehensions I felt from

what you said of the Queen's being ill, though you added the news of her being recovered, gave my carcase a very ugly shock: so much do my own fears naturally outweigh my joys, or plainer, so much am I rather a coward than a hero. Good God! what a thousand things have I thought, since I received your letter, if that should happen, which one hates even to think of, what is to become of us? What sort or set of men are to be our taskmasters? and what sluices are we provided with, to save Great Britain from being overflowed? after what would become of us all? the thought, I grant you, is very mean, what would become of me? But humanity is frail and querulous. If the prospect, therefore, of this evil, though, I hope, far removed, be dreadful to the masters of Mortimer Castle, Hinton St. George, Stanton Harcourt, or Bucklebury, what must it be to friend Matt, qui oppressus inimicis et invidia, ærumnis et paupertate, morbis et annis, or, as it is upon the tombstone, since goods, sine lands, sine riches? Why wont Lord Treasurer think of this one half hour, since we may do it at any half hour, since he intends to do it, I believe: and possibly, half an hour too late, will be as sorry as myself that it was not done? But if the Queen is well, hang all the rest. Gaultier had alarmed this court; upon your letter I was glad to convince them that there was no ground for their apprehensions, your Lordship's letter giving so good an account of her majesty's indisposition being so happily past. And accordingly I continued the appointment and invitation I had made to some of our friends to dine with me yesterday. Monsieur could not, as he promised, come, the king having appointed him to wait on his majesty at Monti. But I had women, Croissy, Torcy, Bouzolles, and (as Madame Croissy had invited her Lady Jersey) men, Card. Polignac, Abbé Pompone, Count Croissy, and that gang. Albergetti to sing accompagnement de musique, and every thing à l'honneur de l'Angleterre. But under this mask of mirth—premit alto corde dolorem—till I hear from England more particularly, that the Queen's health is confirmed, &c.

1714, April.—By what I have sent you inclosed, I hope, my dear Lord Bolingbroke, I shall hear no more of sluices "till Shiloh comes." What are ye all doing in England, and (as these people ask me) who are the government? For my own part, I hear nothing from that merry island, but that you, I, and all our friends are called rogues and rascals all the day long, and in every coffee-house. Quousque tandem? &c.

MY DEAR LORD AND FRIEND, May 1, 1714.

MATTHEW had never so great an occasion to write a word to Henry as now; it is noised here that I am soon to return. The question that I wish I could answer to the many that ask, and to our friend Colbert de Torcy (to whom I made your compliments in the manner you commanded) is, what is done for me, and to what I am recalled? It may look like a bagatelle, what is to become of a philosopher like me: but it is not such, what is to become of a person who had the honour to be chosen and sent hither, as intrusted in the midst of a war, with what the queen designed should make the peace. Returning with the Lord Bolingbroke, one of the greatest men in England, and one of the finest heads in Europe (as they say here, if true or not, n'importe) having been left by him in the greatest character, that of her majesty's plenipotentiary, exercising that power conjointly with the Duke of Shrewsbury, and solely after his departure. Having here received more distinguished honour than any minister, except an ambassador, ever did; and some which were never given to any, but who had that character; having had all the success that could be expected, having (God be thanked) spared no pains at a time, when the peace at home is voted safe and honourable, at a time when the Earl of Oxford is lord treasurer, and Lord Bolingbroke first secretary of state; this unfortunate person, I say, neglected, forgot, unnamed to any thing that may speak the queen satisfied with his services, or his friends concerned as to his fortune. Monsieur de Torcy put me quite out of countenance the other day, by a pity that wounded me deeper than ever did the cruelty of the late Lord Godolphin. He said he would write to Robin and Harry about me. God forbid, my lord, that I should need any foreign intercession, or owe the least to any Frenchman living, besides decency of behaviour, and the returns of common civility. Some say I am to go to Baden, others, that I am to be added to the commissioners for settling the commerce. In all cases, I am ready, but in the mean time,—*dic aliquid de tribus capillis.* Neither of these two are, I presume, honours or rewards, neither of them (let me say to my dear Lord Bolingbroke, and let him not be angry with me) are what Drift[1] may aspire to, and what Mr. Whitworth, who was his fellow-clerk, has or may possess. I am far from desiring to lessen the great merit of the gentleman I named, for I heartily esteem and love him. But in this trade of ours, my lord, in which you are the general, as in that of the soldiery, there is a certain right acquired by time and long service. You would do any thing for your queen's service, but you would not be contented to descend and be degraded to a charge no way proportioned to that of secretary of state, any more than Mr. Ross, though he would charge a party with a halberd in his hand, would be content all his life after to be a servant. Was my Lord Dartmouth, from secretary returned again to be commissioner of trade, or from secretary of war, would Frank Gwin think himself kindly used to be returned again to be commissioner. In short,

[1] His secretary.

my lord, you have put me above myself, and if I am to return to myself, I shall return to something very discontented and uneasy. I am sure, my lord, you will make the best up you can of this hint for my good. If I am to have any thing, it will certainly be for her majesty's service, and the credit of my friends in the ministry, that it be done before I am recalled from hence, lest the world may think either that I have merited to be disgraced, or that you dare not stand by me: if nothing is to be done *fiat voluntas Dei.* I have writ to Lord Treasurer on this subject, and having implored your kind intercession, I promise you, it is the last remonstrance of the kind I will ever make. Adieu! my Lord! all honour, health and pleasure to you.

Yours ever, MATT.

MY DEAR LORD, 1714, Aug. 7.

I SHOULD be wanting in my duty and friendship to you, if I were silent upon a point, which for me, of all men, it is most dangerous to touch: you will easily guess it is the differences, and as they are represented here, the open quarrels between my masters at Whitehall. Who is in the wrong, or who is in the right, is not in my power at this distance to determine; but this thing, every one sees at this court, from Torcy to Courtenvaux, as I believe they do in yours, from my Lord Chancellor to Miramont, that the honour of our nation daily diminishes, and the credit of the ministers most particularly suffers. I would expatiate upon this topic, if I did not write to a man of your superior sense, and I need make no excuse for touching upon it, because, I am sure, I write to a man who loves me and knows I love him. I have one reason to wish an end to these misunderstandings, more than any man else, which is, that I foresee my own ruin inevitably fixed in their continuance; but be all that as it will, my Lord Bolingbroke shall never be ashamed of my conduct, or find me behave otherwise than as an honest and an English man.

Am I to go to Fontainbleau? am I to come here? am I to be looked upon? am I to hang myself? From the present prospect of things, the latter begins to look most elegible. Adieu! my Lord, God bless you! I am ever inviolably yours,

MATT.

Mons. de Torcy has very severe, and I fear very exact accounts of us; we are all frightened out of our wits, upon the Duke of Marlborough's going into England.

THE POEMS OF PRIOR.

TO THE

RIGHT HONOURABLE LIONEL, EARL OF DORSET AND MIDDLESEX.*

It looks like no great compliment to your Lordship, that I prefix your name to this epistle; when, in the preface, I declare the book is published almost against my inclination. But, in all cases, my Lord, you have an hereditary right to whatever may be called mine. Many of the following pieces were written by the command of your excellent father; and most of the rest, under his protection and patronage.

The particular felicity of your birth, my Lord; the natural endowments of your mind, which, without suspicion of flattery, I may tell you, are very great; the good education with which these parts have been improved; and your coming into the world, and seeing men very early; make us expect from your Lordship all the good, which our hopes can form in favour of a young nobleman. *Tu Marcellus eris*,—Our eyes and our hearts are turned on you. You must be a judge and master of polite learning; a friend and patron to men of

* Afterwards created Duke of Dorset.

letters and merit; a faithful and able counsellor to your prince; a true patriot to your country; an ornament and honour to the titles you possess; and, in one word, a worthy son to the great Earl of Dorset.[1]

It is as impossible to mention that name, without desiring to commend the person, as it is to give him the commendations which his virtues de-

[1] Born 24 January, 1637, died 29 January, 1705–6. Mr. Walpole observes that "he was the finest gentleman in the voluptuous court of Charles the Second, and in the gloomy one of King William: he had as much wit as his first master, or his contemporaries, Buckingham and Rochester, without the royal want of feeling, the Duke's want of principles, or the Earl's want of thought. The latter said with astonishment, 'That he did not know how it was, but Lord Dorset might do any thing, and yet was never to blame.'—It was not that he was free from the failings of humanity, but he had the tenderness of it too, which made every body excuse whom every body loved, for even the asperity of his verses seems to have been forgiven to 'The best good of man, with the worst natur'd Muse.'—This line is not more familiar than Lord Dorset's own poems, to all who have a taste for the genteelest beauties of natural and easy verse, or than his Lordship's own bon mots; of which I cannot help repeating one of singular humour. Lord Craven was a proverb for officious whispers to men in power. On Lord Dorset's promotion, King Charles having seen Lord Craven pay his usual tribute to him, asked the former what the latter had been saying: the Earl replied gravely, 'Sir, my Lord Craven did me the honour to whisper, but I did not think it good manners to listen.' When he was dying, Congreve, who had been to visit him, being asked how he had left him, replied, 'faith, he slabbers more wit than other people do in their best health.'" Catalogue of Royal and Noble Authors, vol. ii. p. 96.

served. But I assure myself, the most agreeable compliment I can bring your Lordship, is to pay a grateful respect to your father's memory. And my own obligations to him were such, that the world must pardon my endeavouring at his character, however I may miscarry in the attempt.

A thousand ornaments and graces met in the composition of this great man, and contributed to make him universally beloved and esteemed. The figure of his body was strong, proportionable, beautiful: and was his picture well drawn, it must deserve the praise given to the portraits of Raphael; and, at once, create love and respect. While the greatness of his mien informed men, they were approaching the nobleman, the sweetness of it invited them to come nearer to the patron. There was in his look and gesture something that is more easily conceived than described; that gained upon you in his favour, before he spake one word. His behaviour was easy and courteous to all; but distinguished and adapted to each man in particular, according to his station and quality. His civility was free from the formality of rule, and flowed immediately from his good sense.

Such were the natural faculties and strength of his mind, that he had occasion to borrow very little from education; and he owed those advantages to his own good parts, which others acquire by study and imitation. His wit was abundant, noble, bold Wit in most writers is like a fountain in a garden supplied by several streams brought through artful pipes, and playing sometimes agreeably. But the Earl of Dorset's was a source rising from the top of a mountain, which forced its own way, and with inexhaustible supplies, delighted and enriched the country through which it passed. This extraordinary genius was accompanied with so true a judgment in all parts of fine learning, that whatever subject was before him, he discoursed as properly of it, as if the peculiar bent of his study had been applied that way; and he perfected his judgment by reading and digesting the best authors, though he quoted them very seldom,

Contemnebat potiùs literas, quàm nesciebat:

and rather seemed to draw his knowledge from his own stores, than to owe it to any foreign assistance.

The brightness of his parts, the solidity of his judgment, and the candour and generosity of his temper distinguished him in an age of great politeness, and at a court abounding with men of the finest sense and learning. The most eminent masters in their several ways appealed to his determination. Waller thought it an honour to consult him in the softness and harmony of his verse: and Dr. Sprat, in the delicacy and turn of his prose. Dryden determines by him,[1] under the character of

[1] See Dryden's Essay on Dramatic Poesie, first printed in quarto, and addressed to Charles Earl of Dorset, then Lord Buckhurst.

Eugenius, as to the laws of dramatic poetry. Butler owed it to him that the court tasted his Hudibras; Wycherley that the town liked his Plain Dealer; and the late Duke of Buckingham deferred to publish his Rehearsal, till he was sure (as he expressed it) that my Lord Dorset would not *rehearse* upon him again. If we wanted foreign testimony, La Fontaine and St. Evremont have acknowledged, that he was a perfect master of the beauty and fineness of their language, and of all that they call *les Belles Lettres*. Nor was this nicety of his judgment confined only to books and literature, but was the same in statuary, painting, and all other parts of art. Bernini would have taken his opinion upon the beauty and attitude of a figure; and King Charles did not agree with Lely, that my Lady Cleveland's picture was finished, till it had the approbation of my Lord Buckhurst.

As the judgment which he made of others' writings could not be refuted, the manner in which he wrote will hardly ever be equalled. Every one of his pieces is an ingot of gold, intrinsically and solidly valuable; such as, wrought or beaten thinner, would shine through a whole book of any other author. His thought was always new; and the expression of it so particularly happy, that every body knew immediately, it could only be my Lord Dorset's: and yet it was so easy too, that every body was ready to imagine himself capable of writing it. There is a lustre in his verses, like that of the sun in Claude Lorraine's landscapes: it looks natural, and is inimitable. His love-verses have a mixture of delicacy and strength: they convey the wit of Petronius in the softness of Tibullus. His satire indeed is so severely pointed, that in it he appears, what his great friend the Earl of Rochester (that other prodigy of the age) says he was;

> The best good man, with the worst natur'd Muse.

Yet even here, that character may justly be applied to him, which Persius gives of the best writer in this kind, that ever lived:

> Omne vafer vitium ridenti Flaccus amico
> Tangit, et admissus circum præcordia ludit.

And the gentleman had always so much the better of the satirist, that the persons touched did not know where to fix their resentments; and were forced to appear rather ashamed than angry. Yet so far was this great author from valuing himself upon his works, that he cared not what became of them, though every body else did. There are many things of his not extant in writing, which however are always repeated: like the verses and sayings of the ancient Druids, they retain an universal veneration, though they are preserved only by memory.

As it is often seen, that those men who are least qualified for business, love it most; my Lord Dorset's character was, that he certainly understood it, but did not care for it.

Coming very young to the possession of two plentiful estates, and in an age when pleasure was more in fashion than business, he turned his parts rather to books and conversation than to politics, and what more immediately related to the public. But whenever the safety of his country demanded his assistance, he readily entered into the most active parts of life, and underwent the greatest dangers with a constancy of mind which showed, that he had not only read the rules of philosophy, but understood the practice of them.

In the first Dutch war he went a volunteer under the Duke of York: his behaviour, during that campaign, was such as distinguished the Sackville descended from that Hildebrand of the name, who was one of the greatest captains that came into England with the Conqueror. But his making a song[1] the night before the engagement (and it was one of the prettiest that ever was made) carries with it so sedate a presence of mind, and such an unusual gallantry, that it deserves as much to be recorded, as Alexander's jesting with his soldiers, before he passed the Granicus; or William the First of Orange, giving order over night for a battle, and desiring to be called in the morning, lest he should happen to sleep too long.

From hence, during the remaining part of King Charles's reign, he continued to live in honourable

[1] The song, beginning, "To all you ladies now at land," is printed in the works of the Minor Poets.

leisure. He was of the bed-chamber to the king, and possessed not only his master's favour, but (in a great degree) his familiarity; never leaving the court, but when he was sent to that of France, on some short commissions and embassies of compliment: as if the king designed to show the French (who would be thought the politest nation), that one of the finest gentlemen in Europe was his subject; and that we had a prince who understood his worth so well, as not to suffer him to be long out of his presence.

The succeeding reign neither relished my Lord's wit, nor approved his maxims: so he retired altogether from court. But as the irretrievable mistakes of that unhappy government went on to threaten the nation with something more terrible than a Dutch war, he thought it became him to resume the courage of his youth, and once more to engage himself in defending the liberty of his country. He entered into the Prince of Orange's interest, and carried on his part of that great enterprise here in London, and under the eye of the court, with the same resolution, as his friend and fellow-patriot, the late Duke of Devonshire, did in open arms at Nottingham, till the dangers of those times increased to extremity, and just apprehensions arose for the safety of the princess, our present glorious queen: then the Earl of Dorset was thought the properest guide of her necessary flight, and the person under whose courage and direction the nation might most safely trust a charge so precious and important.

After the establishment of their late majesties upon the throne, there was room again at court for men of my Lord's character. He had a part in the councils of those princes, a great share in their friendship, and all the marks of distinction with which a good government could reward a patriot. He was made chamberlain of their majesties' household, a place which he so eminently adorned by the grace of his person, the fineness of his breeding, and the knowledge and practice of what was decent and magnificent, that he could only be rivalled in these qualifications by one great man, who has since held the same staff.

The last honours he received from his sovereign (and indeed they were the greatest which a subject could receive), were, that he was made knight of the garter, and constituted one of the regents of the kingdom, during his majesty's absence. But his health, about that time, sensibly declining, and the public affairs not threatened by any imminent danger, he left the business to those who delighted more in the state of it, and appeared only sometimes at council, to show his respect to the commission; giving as much leisure as he could to the relief of those pains, with which it pleased God to afflict him, and indulging the reflections of a mind, that had looked through the world with too piercing an eye, and was grown weary of the prospect. Upon the whole, it may very justly be said of this great man, with regard to the public, that through the course of his life, he acted like an able pilot in a long voyage; contented to sit quiet in the cabin, when the winds were allayed, and the waters smooth; but vigilant and ready to resume the helm, when the storm arose, and the sea grew tumultuous.

I ask your pardon, my Lord, if I look yet a little more nearly into the late Lord Dorset's character: if I examine it not without some intention of finding fault; and (which is an odd way of making a panegyric) set his blemishes and imperfections in open view.

The fire of his youth carried him to some excesses, but they were accompanied with a most lively invention, and true humour. The little violences and easy mistakes of a night too gaily spent (and that too in the beginning of life), were always set right the next day, with great humanity, and ample retribution. His faults brought their excuse with them, and his very failings had their beauties. So much sweetness accompanied what he said, and so great generosity what he did, that people were always prepossessed in his favour; and it was in fact true, what the late Earl of Rochester said in jest to King Charles, that he did not know how it was, but my Lord Dorset might do any thing, yet was never to blame.

He was naturally very subject to passion; but the short gust was soon over, and served only to set off the charms of his temper, when more composed. That very passion broke out with a force of wit, which made even anger agreeable: while it lasted, he said and forgot a thousand things, which other men would have been glad to have studied and wrote; but the impetuosity was corrected upon a moment's reflection, and the measure altered with such grace and delicacy, that you could scarce perceive where the key was changed.

He was very sharp in his reflections; but never in the wrong place. His darts were sure to wound; but they were sure too to hit none but those whose follies gave him a very fair aim. And when he allowed no quarter, he had certainly been provoked by more than common error; by men's tedious and circumstantial recitals of their affairs, or by their multiplied questions about his own; by extreme ignorance and impertinence; or the mixture of these, an ill-judged and never-ceasing civility; or lastly, by the two things which were his utter aversion, the insinuation of a flatterer, and the whisper of a tale-bearer.

If, therefore, we set the piece in its worst position; if its faults be most exposed; the shades will still appear very finely joined with their lights; and every imperfection will be diminished by the lustre of some neighbouring virtue. But if we turn the great drawings and wonderful colourings to their true light, the whole must appear beautiful, noble, admirable.

He possessed all those virtues in the highest degree, upon which the pleasure of society, and the happiness of life depend; and he exercised them with the greatest decency and best manners. As good nature is said, by a great[1] author, to belong more particularly to the English than any other nation, it may again be said, that it belonged more particularly to the late Earl of Dorset than to any other English man.

A kind husband he was, without fondness; and an indulgent father, without partiality. So extraordinary good a master, that this quality ought indeed to have been numbered among his defects, for he was often served worse than became his station, from his unwillingness to assume an authority too severe. And during those little transports of passion, to which I just now said he was subject, I have known his servants get into his way, that they might make a merit of it immediately after; for he that had the good fortune to be chid, was sure of being rewarded for it.

His table was one of the last that gave us an example of the old housekeeping of an English nobleman. A freedom reigned at it, which made every one of his guests think himself at home; and an abundance, which showed that the master's hospitality extended to many more than those who had the honour to sit at table with him.

In his dealings with others, his care and ex-

[1] Sprat, Hist. of the Royal Society.

actness that every man should have his due, was such that you would think he had never seen a court: the politeness and civility with which this justice was administered, would convince you he never had lived out of one.

He was so strict an observer of his word, that no consideration whatever could make him break it; yet so cautious, lest the merit of his act should arise from that obligation only, that he usually did the greatest favours without making any previous promise. So inviolable was he in his friendship, and so kind to the character of those whom he had once honoured with a more intimate acquaintance, that nothing less than a demonstration of some essential fault could make him break with them; and then too, his good nature did not consent to it, without the greatest reluctance and difficulty. Let me give one instance of this amongst many. When, as lord chamberlain, he was obliged to take the king's pension from Mr. Dryden, who had long before put himself out of a possibility of receiving any favour from the court, my Lord allowed him an equivalent out of his own estate. However displeased with the conduct of his old acquaintance, he relieved his necessities; and while he gave him his assistance in private, in public he extenuated and pitied his error.

The foundation indeed of these excellent qualities, and the perfection of my Lord Dorset's character, was that unbounded charity which ran through the whole tenor of his life, and sat as visibly predominant over the other faculties of his soul, as she is said to do in Heaven, above her sister virtues.

Crowds of poor daily thronged his gates, expecting thence their bread; and were still lessened by his sending the most proper objects of his bounty to apprenticeships, or hospitals. The lazar and the sick, as he accidentally saw them, were removed from the street to the physician; and many of them not only restored to health, but supplied with what might enable them to resume their former callings, and make their future life happy. The prisoner has often been released, by my Lord's paying the debt; and the condemned has been saved by his intercession with the sovereign, where he thought the letter of the law too rigid. To those whose circumstances were such as made them ashamed of their poverty, he knew how to bestow his munificence without offending their modesty; and under the notion of frequent presents, gave them what amounted to a subsistence. Many yet alive know this to be true, though he told it to none, nor ever was more uneasy than when any one mentioned it to him.

We may find among the Greeks and Latins, Tibullus and Gallus, the noblemen that writ poetry; Augustus and Mæcenas, the protectors of learning; Aristides, the good citizen; and Atticus, the well-bred friend; and bring them in, as examples of my

Lord Dorset's wit, his judgment, his justice, and his civility. But for his charity, my Lord, we can scarce find a parallel in history itself.

Titus was not more the *deliciæ humani generis*, on this account, than my Lord Dorset was; and, without any exaggeration, that prince did not do more good in proportion out of the revenue of the Roman empire, than your father out of the income of a private estate. Let this, my Lord, remain to you and your posterity a possession for ever; to be imitated, and, if possible, to be excelled.

As to my own particular, I scarce knew what life was, sooner than I found myself obliged to his favour; nor have had reason to feel any sorrow so sensibly as that of his death.

> "Ille dies—quem semper acerbum
> Semper honoratum (sic Dî voluistis) habebo."

Æneas could not reflect upon the loss of his own father with greater piety, my Lord, than I must recall the memory of yours: and when I think whose son I am writing to, the least I promise myself from your goodness is an uninterrupted continuance of favour, and a friendship for life. To which, that I may with some justice entitle myself, I send your Lordship a dedication, not filled with a long detail of your praises, but with my sincerest wishes that you may deserve them. That you may employ those extraordinary parts and abilities with which heaven has blessed you, to the honour of your family, the benefit of your friends, and the good of your country; that all your actions may be great, open, and noble, such as may tell the world whose son and whose successor you are.

What I now offer to your Lordship is a collection of poetry, a kind of garland of good-will. If any verses of my writing should appear in print, under another name and patronage, than that of an Earl of Dorset, people might suspect them not to be genuine. I have attained my present end, if these poems prove the diversion of some of your youthful hours, as they have been occasionally the amusement of some of mine; and I humbly hope, that as I may hereafter bind up my fuller sheaf, and lay some pieces of a very different nature (the product of my severer studies) at your Lordship's feet, I shall engage your more serious reflection: happy, if in all my endeavours I may contribute to your delight or to your instruction. I am, with all duty and respect,

My Lord,

Your Lordship's most obedient, and

Most humble Servant,

MAT. PRIOR.

PREFACE.

THE greatest part of what I have written having been already published, either singly or in some of the miscellanies, it would be too late for me to make any excuse for appearing in print. But a collection of poems has lately appeared under my name, though without my knowledge, in which the publisher has given me the honour of some things that did not belong to me; and has transcribed others so imperfectly, that I hardly knew them to be mine. This has obliged me, in my own defence, to look back upon some of those lighter studies, which I ought long since to have quitted, and to publish an indifferent collection of poems, for fear of being thought the author of a worse.

Thus I beg pardon of the public for reprinting some pieces, which as they came singly from their first impression, have (I fancy) lain long and quietly in Mr. Tonson's shop; and adding others to them, which were never before printed, and might have lain as quietly, and perhaps more safely, in a corner of my own study.

The reader will, I hope, make allowance for their having been written at very distant times, and on very different occasions, and take them as they happen to come. Public panegyrics, amorous odes, serious reflections, or idle tales, the product of his leisure hours, who had business enough upon his hands, and was only a poet by accident.

I own myself obliged to Mrs. Singer, who has given me leave to print a pastoral of her writing; that poem having produced the verses immediately following it. I wish she might be prevailed with to publish some other pieces of that kind, in which the softness of her sex, and the fineness of her genius, conspire to give her a very distinguishing character.

POSTSCRIPT.

I must help my preface by a postscript, to tell the reader, that there are ten years distance between my writing the one and the other; and that (whatever I thought then, and have somewhere said, that I would publish no more poetry) he will find several copies of verses scattered through this edition, which were not printed in the first. Those relating to the public stand in the order they did before, and according to the several years in which they were written, however the disposition of our national affairs, the actions, or the fortunes of some men, and the opinions of others may have changed. Prose, and other human things may take what turn they can; but poetry, which pretends to have something of divinity in it, is to be more permanent. Odes once printed cannot well be altered, when the author has already said, that he expects his works should live for ever. And it had been very foolish in my friend Horace, if some years after his Exegi Monumentum, he should have desired to see his building taken down again.

The dedication, likewise, is reprinted to the Earl of Dorset, in the foregoing leaves, without any alteration; though I had the fairest opportunity, and the strongest inclination to have added a great deal to it. The blooming hopes, which I said the world expected from my then very young patron, have been confirmed by most noble and distinguished first-fruits; and his life is going on towards a plentiful harvest of all accumulated virtues. He has in fact exceeded whatever the fondness of my wishes could invent in his favour: his equally good and beautiful lady enjoys in him an indulgent and obliging husband; his children, a kind and careful father; and his acquaintance, a faithful, generous, and polite friend. His fellow peers have attended to the persuasion of his eloquence; and have been convinced by the solidity of his reasoning. He has long since deserved and attained the honour of the garter. He has managed some of the greatest charges of the kingdom with known ability; and laid them down with entire disinterestment. And as he continues the exercises of these eminent virtues (which that he may do to a very old age, shall be my perpetual wish) he may be one of the greatest men that our age, or possibly our nation has bred; and leave materials for a panegyric, not unworthy the pen of some future Pliny.

From so noble a subject as the Earl of Dorset, to so mean a one as myself, is (I confess) a very pindaric transition. I shall only say one word, and trouble the reader no farther. I published my poems formerly, as Monsieur Jourdain sold his silk: he would not be thought a tradesman, but ordered some pieces to be measured out to his particular friends. Now I give up my shop, and dispose of all my poetical goods at once: I must therefore desire, that the public would please to take them in the gross; and that every body would turn over what he does not like.

THE

POEMS OF MATTHEW PRIOR.

ON EXOD. III. 14.—I AM THAT I AM.

AN ODE. WRITTEN IN 1688, AS AN EXERCISE AT ST. JOHN'S COLLEGE, CAMBRIDGE.

MAN! foolish man!
Scarce know'st thou how thyself began;
Scarce hast thou thought enough to prove thou art;
Yet, steel'd with studied boldness, thou dar'st try
To send thy doubting reason's dazzled eye
Through the mysterious gulf of vast immensity.
Much thou canst there discern, much thence impart.
Vain wretch! suppress thy knowing pride;
Mortify thy learned lust!
Vain are thy thoughts, while thou thyself art dust.

Let Wit her sails, her oars let Wisdom lend;
The helm let politic Experience guide:
Yet cease to hope thy short-liv'd bark shall ride
Down spreading Fate's unnavigable tide.
What, though still it farther tend?
Still 'tis farther from its end;
And, in the bosom of that boundless sea,
Still finds its error lengthen with its way.

With daring pride and insolent delight
Your doubts resolv'd you boast, your labours
crown'd;
And ʽΕΥΡΗΚΑ! your god, forsooth is found
Incomprehensible and infinite.
But is he therefore found? vain searcher! no:
Let your imperfect definition show
That nothing you, the weak definer, know.

Say, why should the collected main
Itself within itself contain?
Why to its caverns should it sometimes creep,
And with delighted silence sleep
On the lov'd bosom of its parent deep?
Why should its numerous waters stay
In comely discipline, and fair array,
Till winds and tides exert their high command?
Then prompt and ready to obey,
Why do the rising surges spread
Their op'ning ranks o'er earth's submissive head,
Marching through different paths to different lands?

Why does the constant sun
With measur'd steps his radiant journeys run?
Why does he order the diurnal hours
To leave earth's other part, and rise on ours?
Why does he wake the correspondent moon,
And fill her willing lamp with liquid light,
Commanding her with delegated powers
To beautify the world, and bless the night?

Why does each animated star
Love the just limits of its proper sphere?
Why does each consenting sign
With prudent harmony combine
In turns to move, and subsequent appear,
To gird the globe, and regulate the year?

Man does with dangerous curiosity
These unfathom'd wonders try:
With fancied rules and arbitrary laws
Matter and motion he restrains;
And studied lines and fictious circles draws:
Then with imagin'd sovereignty
Lord of his new hypothesis he reigns.
He reigns: how long? till some usurper rise;
And he too, mighty thoughtful, mighty wise,
Studies new lines, and other circles feigns.
From this last toil again what knowledge flows?
Just as much, perhaps, as shows,
That all his predecessor's rules
Were empty cant, all jargon of the schools;
That he on t'other's ruin rears his throne;
And shows his friend's mistake, and thence confirms his own.

On earth, in air, amidst the seas and skies,
Mountainous heaps of wonders rise;
Whose towering strength will ne'er submit
To Reason's batteries, or the mines of wit:
Yet still inquiring, still mistaking man,

Each hour repuls'd, each hour dare onward press:
And levelling at God his wandering guess,
(That feeble engine of his reasoning war,
Which guides his doubts, and combats his despair)
Laws to his Maker the learn'd wretch can give:
Can bound that nature, and prescribe that will,
Whose pregnant word did either ocean fill:
Can tell us whence all beings are, and how they move and live.
Through either ocean, foolish man!
That pregnant word sent forth again,
Might to a world extend each atom there;
For every drop call forth a sea, a heaven for every star.

Let cunning Earth her fruitful wonders hide;
And only lift thy staggering reason up
To trembling Calvary's astonish'd top;
Then mock thy knowledge, and confound thy pride,
Explaining how Perfection suffer'd pain,
Almighty languish'd, and Eternal died:
How by her patient victor Death was slain;
And earth profan'd, yet bless'd with Deicide.
Then down with all thy boasted volumes, down;
Only reserve the sacred one:
Low, reverently low,
Make thy stubborn knowledge bow;
Weep out thy reason's, and thy body's eyes;
Deject thyself, that thou may'st rise;
To look to Heaven, be blind to all below.

Then Faith, for Reason's glimmering light, shall give
Her immortal perspective;
And Grace's presence Nature's loss retrieve.
Then thy enliven'd soul shall see,
That all the volumes of philosophy,
With all their comments, never could invent
So politic an instrument,
To reach the Heaven of Heavens, the high abode,
Where Moses places his mysterious God,
As was that ladder which old Jacob rear'd,
When light divine had human darkness clear'd;
And his enlarg'd ideas found the road,
Which faith had dictated, and Angels trod.

TO THE COUNTESS OF EXETER,[1]

PLAYING ON THE LUTE.

What charms you have, from what high race you sprung,
Have been the pleasing subjects of my song:

[1] Anne, daughter of William Earl of Devonshire, and sister to the first Duke of Devonshire, widow also to Charles Lord Rich, was married to John Cecil Lord Burleigh, afterwards Earl of Exeter; she attended her lord upon all his travels, and was present when he died, August 29, 1700, at a village called Issy, near Paris, and surviving him till the 18th June, 1703, the remains of both were deposited at St. Martin, Stamford, where a magnificent monument, brought among other curious works from Rome, is erected to their memory.

Unskill'd and young, yet something still I writ,
Of Ca'ndish' beauty join'd to Cecil's wit.
But when you please to show the lab'ring Muse,
What greater theme your music can produce;
My babbling praises I repeat no more,
But hear, rejoice, stand silent, and adore.
  The Persians thus, first gazing on the sun,
Admir'd how high 'twas plac'd, how bright it shone;
But, as his power was known, their thoughts were
    rais'd;
And soon they worshipp'd, what at first they prais'd.
  Eliza's glory lives in Spenser's song;
And Cowley's verse keeps fair Orinda young.
That as in birth, in beauty you excel,
The Muse might dictate, and the Poet tell:
Your art no other art can speak; and you,
To show how well you play, must play anew:
[1] Your music's power your music must disclose;
For what light is, 'tis only light that shows.
  Strange force of harmony, that thus controls
Our thoughts, and turns and sanctifies our souls:
While with its utmost art your sex could move
Our wonder only, or at best our love:
You far above both these your God did place,
That your high power might worldly thoughts de-
    stroy;

1 Imitated from Alleyne's Poetical History of Henry VII.

"For nought but light itself, itself can show,
And only kings can write what kings can do."

That with your numbers you our zeal might raise,
And, like himself, communicate your joy.
When to your native Heaven you shall repair,
And with your presence crown the blessings there,
Your lute may wind its strings but little higher,
To tune their notes to that immortal quire.
Your art is perfect here; your numbers do,
More than our books, make the rude atheist know,
That there's a Heaven, by what he hears below.
As in some piece, while Luke his skill exprest,
A cunning angel came, and drew the rest:
So, when you play, some godhead does impart
Harmonious aid, divinity helps art;
Some cherub finishes what you begun,
And to a miracle improves a tune.
To burning Rome when frantic Nero play'd,
Viewing that face, no more he had survey'd
The raging flames; but, struck with strange surprise,
Confest them less than those of Anna's eyes:
But, had he heard thy lute, he soon had found
His rage eluded, and his crime aton'd:
Thine, like Amphion's hand, had wak'd the stone,
And from destruction call'd the rising town:
Malice to Music had been forc'd to yield;
Nor could he burn so fast, as thou couldst build.

PICTURE OF SENECA DYING IN A BATH.

BY JORDAIN.[1] AT THE RIGHT HON. THE EARL OF EXETER'S, AT BURLEIGH HOUSE.

WHILE cruel Nero only drains
The moral Spaniard's ebbing veins,
By study worn, and slack with age,
How dull, how thoughtless is his rage!
Heighten'd revenge he should have took;
He should have burnt his tutor's book;
And long have reign'd supreme in vice:
One nobler wretch can only rise;
'Tis he whose fury shall deface
The stoic's image in this piece.

[1] Jacques Jordain was born at Antwerp in 1584; was a disciple of Adam van Oort, but was indebted to Rubens for the principal part of his knowledge in the art of painting: "He painted with extraordinary freedom, ease, and expedition; there is a brilliancy and harmony in his colouring, and a good understanding of the Chiaroscuro. His composition is rich, his expression natural and strong, but his design wanted elegance and taste. He studied and copied nature, yet he neither selected its beauties, nor rejected its defects. He knew how to give his figures a good relief, though frequently incorrect in the outlines; but his pencil is always excellent, and for a free and spirited touch, no painter can be accounted his superior." Pilkington's Dictionary of Painters. He died in 1678, aged 84 years.

For while unhurt, divine Jordain,
Thy work and Seneca's remain,
He still has body, still has soul,
And lives and speaks, restor'd and whole.

AN ODE.

While blooming youth, and gay delight
  Sit on thy rosy cheeks confest,
Thou hast, my dear, undoubted right
  To triumph o'er this destin'd breast.
My reason bends to what thy eyes ordain:
For I was born to love, and thou to reign.

But would you meanly thus rely
  On power, you know I must obey?
Exert a legal tyranny;
  And do an ill, because you may?
Still must I thee, as atheists Heaven adore;
Not see thy mercy, and yet dread thy power?

Take heed, my dear, youth flies apace;
  As well as Cupid, Time is blind:
Soon must those glories of thy face
  The fate of vulgar beauty find:
The thousand loves, that arm thy potent eye,
Must drop their quivers, flag their wings, and die.

Then wilt thou sigh, when in each frown
A hateful wrinkle more appears;
And putting peevish humours on,
Seems but the sad effect of years:
Kindness itself too weak a charm will prove,
To raise the feeble fires of aged love.

Forc'd compliments and formal bows
Will show thee just above neglect:
The heat with which thy lover glows,
Will settle into cold respect:
A talking dull Platonic I shall turn;
Learn to be civil, when I cease to burn.

Then shun the ill, and know, my dear,
Kindness and constancy will prove
The only pillars fit to bear
So vast a weight as that of love.
If thou canst wish to make my flames endure,
Thine must be very fierce, and very pure.

Haste, Celia, haste, while youth invites,
Obey kind Cupid's present voice;
Fill ev'ry sense with soft delights,
And give thy soul a loose to joys:
Let millions of repeated blisses prove,
That thou all kindness art, and I all love.

Be mine, and only mine; take care
Thy looks, thy thoughts, thy dreams to guide

To me alone; nor come so far,
As liking any youth beside:
What men e'er court thee, fly 'em, and believe,
They're serpents all, and thou the tempted Eve.

So shall I court thy dearest truth,
When beauty ceases to engage;
So thinking on thy charming youth,
I'll love it o'er again in age:
So time itself our raptures shall improve,
While still we wake to joy, and live to love.

AN
EPISTLE TO FLEETWOOD SHEPHERD, ESQ.

BURLEIGH, MAY 14, 1689.

SIR,

As once a twelvemonth to the priest,
Holy at Rome, here antichrist,
The Spanish king presents a jennet,
To show his love;—That's all that's in it:
For if his holiness would thump
His reverend bum 'gainst horse's rump,
He might b' equipt from his own stable
With one more white, and eke more able.
Or as with Gondolas, and men, his
Good excellence the Duke of Venice

(I wish, for rhyme, 't had been the king)
Sails out, and gives the gulf a ring;
Which trick of state, he wisely maintains,
Keeps kindness up 'twixt old acquaintance:
For else, in honest truth, the sea
Has much less need of gold, than he.
Or, not to rove, and pump one's fancy
For popish similes beyond sea;
As folks from mud-wall'd tenement
Bring landlords pepper-corn for rent;
Present a turkey, or a hen
To those might better spare than ten:
Ev'n so, with all submission, I
(For first men instance, then apply)
Send you each year a homely letter,
Who may return me much a better.
Then take it, Sir, as it was writ,
To pay respect, and not show wit:
Nor look askew at what it saith;
There's no petition in it,—'Faith.
Here some would scratch their heads, and try
What they should write, and how, and why;
But I conceive, such folks are quite in
Mistakes, in theory of writing.
If once for principle 'tis laid,
That thought is trouble to the head;
I argue thus: the world agrees,
That he writes well, who writes with ease:
Then he, by sequel logical,
Writes best, who never thinks at all.

Verse comes from Heav'n, like inward light;
Mere human pains can ne'er come by 't:
The god, not we, the poem makes;
We only tell folks what he speaks.
Hence when anatomists discourse,
How like brutes' organs are to ours;
They grant, if higher powers think fit,
A bear might soon be made a wit;
And that for any thing in nature,
Pigs might squeak love-odes, dogs bark satire.
Memnon, though stone, was counted vocal;
But 'twas the god, meanwhile, that spoke all.
Rome oft has heard a cross haranguing,
With prompting priest behind the hanging:
The wooden head resolv'd the question;
While you and Pettis help'd the jest on.
Your crabbed rogues, that read Lucretius
Are against gods, you know ; and teach us,
The god makes not the poet; but
The thesis, vice-versâ put,
Should Hebrew-wise be understood;
And means, the poet makes the god.
Egyptian gard'ners thus are said to
Have set the leeks they after pray'd to ;
And Romish bakers praise the deity
They chipp'd, while yet in its paniety.
That when you poets swear and cry,
The god inspires; I rave, I die;
If inward wind does truly swell ye,
'T must be the colic in your belly:

That writing is but just like dice;
And lucky maids make people wise:
That jumbled words, if fortune throw 'em,
Shall, well as Dryden, form a poem;
Or make a speech, correct and witty,
As you know who—at the committee.
So atoms dancing round the centre,
They urge, made all things at a venture.
But granting matters should be spoke
By method, rather than by luck;
This may confine their younger styles,
Whom Dryden pedagogues at Will's:
But never could be meant to tie
Authentic wits, like you and I:
For as young children, who are try'd in
Go-carts, to keep their steps from sliding;
When members knit, and legs grow stronger,
Make use of such machine no longer;
But leap *pro libitu*, and scout
On horse call'd hobby, or without:
So when at school we first declaim,
Old Busby walks us in a theme,
Whose props support our infant vein,
And help the rickets in the brain:
But when our souls their force dilate,
And thoughts grow up to wit's estate;
In verse or prose, we write or chat,
Not sixpence matter upon what.
'Tis not how well an author says;
But 'tis how much, that gathers praise.

Tonson, who is himself a wit,
Counts writers' merits by the sheet.
Thus each should down with all he thinks,
As boys eat bread, to fill up chinks.
  Kind Sir, I should be glad to see you;
I hope y' are well; so God be wi' you;
Was all I thought at first to write:
But things, since then, are alter'd quite;
Fancies flew in, and Muse flies high;
So God knows when my clack will lie:
I must, Sir, prattle on, as afore,
And beg your pardon yet this half-hour.
  So at pure barn of loud Non-con,
Where with my grannam I have gone,
When Lobb had sifted all his text,
And I well hop'd the pudding next;
Now TO APPLY, has plagued me more,
Than all his villain cant before.
  For your religion, first, of her
Your friends do sav'ry things aver:
They say, she's honest, as your claret,
Not sour'd with cant, nor stumm'd with merit:
Your chamber is the sole retreat
Of chaplains every Sunday night:
Of grace, no doubt, a certain sign,
When layman herds with man divine:
For if their fame be justly great,
Who would no Popish nuncio treat;
That his is greater, we must grant,
Who will treat nuncios Protestant.

One single positive weighs more,
You know, than negatives a score.
  In politics, I hear, you're stanch,
Directly bent against the French;
Deny to have your free-born toe
Dragoon'd into a wooden shoe:
Are in no plots; but fairly drive at
The public welfare, in your private:
And will, for England's glory, try
Turks, Jews, and Jesuits to defy,
And keep your places till you die.
  For me, whom wand'ring Fortune threw
From what I lov'd, the town and you;
Let me just tell you how my time is
Past in a country-life.—Imprimis,
As soon as Phœbus' rays inspect us,
First, Sir, I read, and then I breakfast;
So on, till foresaid god does set,
I sometimes study, sometimes eat.
Thus, of your heroes and brave boys,
With whom old Homer makes such noise,
The greatest actions I can find,
Are, that they did their work, and din'd.
  The books of which I'm chiefly fond,
Are such, as you have whilom conn'd;
That treat of China's civil law,
And subjects' rights in Golconda;
Of highway-elephants at Ceylan,
That rob in clans, like men o' th' Highland
Of apes that storm, or keep a town,

As well almost as count Lauzun;
Of unicorns and aligators,
Elks, mermaids, mummies, witches, satyrs,
And twenty other stranger matters;
Which, though they're things I've no concern in,
Make all our grooms admire my learning.
  Critics I read on other men,
And hypers upon them again;
From whose remarks I give opinion
On twenty books, yet ne'er look in one.
  Then all your wits, that fleer and sham,
Down from Don Quixote to Tom Tram;
From whom I jests and puns purloin,
And slily put them off for mine:
Fond to be thought a country wit:
The rest,—when fate and you think fit.
  Sometimes I climb my mare, and kick her
To bottled ale, and country vicar;
Sometimes at Stamford take a quart,
Squire Shephard's health,—with all my heart.
  Thus, without much delight, or grief,
I fool away an idle life;
Till Shadwell from the town retires,
(Chok'd up with fame and sea-coal fires),
To bless the wood with peaceful lyric;
Then hey for praise and panegyric;
Justice restor'd, and nations freed,
And wreaths round William's glorious head.

TO THE COUNTESS OF DORSET,

WRITTEN IN HER MILTON, BY MR. BRADBURY.

SEE here how bright the first-born virgin shone,
And how the first fond lover was undone.
Such charming words our beauteous mother spoke,
As Milton wrote, and such as yours her look.
Yours, the best copy of th' original face,
Whose beauty was to furnish all the race:
Such chains no author could escape but he;
There's no way to be safe, but not to see.

TO THE LADY DURSLEY:[1]

ON THE SAME SUBJECT.

HERE reading how fond Adam was betray'd,
And how by sin Eve's blasted charms decay'd;
Our common loss unjustly you complain;
So small that part of it, which you sustain.
  You still, fair mother, in your offspring trace

[1] Elizabeth, daughter of Baptist Noel, Viscount Campden. She died 30 July, 1719. Her husband, Charles Earl of Berkeley (when Lord Dursley), had been envoy extraordinary and plenipotentiary to the States of Holland, from whence he returned in 1695.

The stock of beauty destin'd for the race:
Kind nature, forming them, the pattern took
For Heav'n's first work, and Eve's original look.
  You, happy saint, the serpent's power control:
Scarce any actual guilt defiles your soul:
And hell does o'er that mind vain triumph boast,
Which gains a Heav'n, for earthly Eden lost.
  With virtue strong as yours had Eve been arm'd,
In vain the fruit had blush'd, or serpent charm'd:
Nor had our bliss by penitence been bought;
Nor had frail Adam fall'n, nor Milton wrote.

TO MY LORD BUCKHURST.[1]

VERY YOUNG, PLAYING WITH A CAT.

THE am'rous youth, whose tender breast
Was by his darling cat possest,
Obtain'd of Venus his desire,
Howe'er irregular his fire:
Nature the pow'r of love obey'd:
The cat became a blushing maid;
And, on the happy change, the boy
Employ'd his wonder, and his joy.
  Take care, O beauteous child, take care,
Lest thou prefer so rash a pray'r:

[1] Lionel, afterwards Duke of Dorset, to whom Prior dedicated his poems.

Nor vainly hope, the queen of love
Will e'er thy fav'rite's charms improve.
O quickly from her shrine retreat;
Or tremble for thy darling's fate.
 The queen of love, who soon will see
Her own Adonis live in thee,
Will lightly her first loss deplore;
Will easily forgive the boar:
Her eyes with tears no more will flow;
With jealous rage her breast will glow:
And on her tabby rival's face
She deep will mark her new disgrace.

AN ODE.

WHILE from our looks, fair nymph, you guess
 The secret passions of our mind,
My heavy eyes, you say, confess
 A heart to love and grief inclin'd.

There needs, alas! but little art,
 To have this fatal secret found:
With the same ease you threw the dart,
 'Tis certain you may show the wound.

How can I see you, and not love;
 While you as op'ning east are fair?
While cold as northern blasts you prove;
 How can I love, and not despair?

The wretch in double fetters bound
  Your potent mercy may release:
Soon, if my love but once were crown'd,
  Fair prophetess, my grief would cease.

A SONG.

In vain you tell your parting lover,
You wish fair winds may waft him over.
Alas! what winds can happy prove,
That bear me far from what I love?
Alas! what dangers on the main
Can equal those that I sustain,
From slighted vows, and cold disdain?
  Be gentle, and in pity choose
To wish the wildest tempests loose:
That, thrown again upon the coast,
Where first my shipwreck'd heart was lost,
I may once more repeat my pain;
Once more in dying notes complain
Of slighted vows, and cold disdain.

THE DESPAIRING SHEPHERD.

ALEXIS shunn'd his fellow swains,
Their rural sports, and jocund strains,
  (Heav'n guard us all from Cupid's bow!)
He lost his crook, he left his flocks;
And wand'ring through the lonely rocks,
  He nourish'd endless woe.

The nymphs and shepherds round him came:
His grief some pity, others blame;
  The fatal cause all kindly seek:
He mingled his concern with theirs;
He gave 'em back their friendly tears;
  He sigh'd, but would not speak.

Clorinda came among the rest;
And she too kind concern express'd,
  And ask'd the reason of his woe:
She ask'd, but with an air and mien,
That made it easily foreseen,
  She fear'd too much to know.

The shepherd rais'd his mournful head;
And will you pardon me, he said,
  While I the cruel truth reveal;
Which nothing from my breast should tear;
Which never should offend your ear,
  But that you bid me tell?

'Tis thus I rove, 'tis thus complain,
Since you appear'd upon the plain;
  You are the cause of all my care;
Your eyes ten thousand dangers dart:
Ten thousand torments vex my heart:
  I love, and I despair.

Too much, Alexis, I have heard:
'Tis what I thought; 'tis what I fear'd:
  And yet I pardon you, she cried:
But you shall promise ne'er again
To breathe your vows, or speak your pain:
  He bow'd, obey'd, and died.

TO

THE HONOURABLE CHARLES MONTAGUE.[1]

HOWE'ER, 'tis well, that while mankind
  Through Fate's perverse meander errs,
He can imagin'd pleasures find,
  To combat against real cares.

[1] Afterwards Earl of Halifax. "He raised himself," says Mr. Walpole, "by his abilities and eloquence in the House of Commons, where he had the honour of being attacked, in conjunction with Lord Somers, and the satisfaction of establishing his innocence as clearly. Addison has celebrated this lord in his account of the greatest English poets: Steele has drawn his character in the dedication of the

Fancies and notions he pursues,
  Which ne'er had being but in thought:
Each, like the Grecian artist,[1] woos
  The image he himself has wrought.

Against experience he believes;
  He argues against demonstration;
Pleas'd, when his reason he deceives;
  And sets his judgment by his passion.

The hoary fool, who many days
  Has struggled with continued sorrow,
Renews his hope, and blindly lays
  The desp'rate bet upon to-morrow.

To-morrow comes: 'tis noon, 'tis night;
  This day like all the former flies:
Yet on he runs, to seek delight
  To-morrow, till to-night he dies.

Our hopes, like tow'ring falcons, aim
  At objects in an airy height:
The little pleasure of the game
  Is from afar to view the flight.

second volume of the Spectator, and the fourth of the Tatler; but Pope in the Portrait of Bufo, in the Epistle to Arbuthnot, has returned the ridicule, which his lordship, in conjunction with Prior, had heaped on Dryden's Hind and Panther." He died 19th May, 1715.

[1] Apelles.

Our anxious pains we, all the day,
In search of what we like, employ:
Scorning at night the worthless prey,
We find the labour gave the joy.

At distance through an artful glass
To the mind's eye things well appear:
They lose their forms, and make a mass
Confus'd and black if brought too near.

If we see right, we see our woes:
Then what avails it to have eyes?
From ignorance our comfort flows.
The only wretched are the wise.

We wearied should lie down in death:
This cheat of life would take no more;
If you thought fame but empty breath;
I, Phillis, but a perjur'd whore.

VARIATIONS IN A COPY PRINTED 1692.

Our hopes, like towering falcons, aim
At objects in an airy height;
But all the pleasure of the game
Is afar off to view the flight.

The worthless prey but only shews
The joy consisted in the strife;

Whate'er we take, as soon we lose
  In Homer's riddle and in life.

So, whilst in feverish sleeps we think
  We taste what waking we desire,
The dream is better than the drink,
  Which only feeds the sickly fire.

To the mind's eye things well appear,
  At distance through an artful glass;
Bring but the flattering objects near,
  They're all a senseless gloomy mass.

Seeing aright, we see our woes:
  Then what avails it to have eyes?
From ignorance our comfort flows,
  The only wretched are the wise.

We wearied should lie down in death,
  This cheat of life would take no more;
If you thought fame but stinking breath,
  And Phyllis but a perjur'd whore.

HYMN TO THE SUN.

SET BY DR. PURCELL,

AND INTENDED TO BE SUNG BEFORE THEIR MAJESTIES ON NEW-YEAR'S DAY, 1693-4. WRITTEN AT THE HAGUE.

LIGHT of the world, and ruler of the year,
With happy speed begin thy great career;
And, as thou dost thy radiant journeys run,
Through every distant climate own,
That in fair Albion thou hast seen
The greatest prince, the brightest queen,
That ever sav'd a land, or blest a throne,
Since first thy beams were spread, or genial power
was known.

So may thy godhead be confest,
So the returning year be blest,
As his infant months bestow
Springing wreaths for William's brow;
As his summer's youth shall shed
Eternal sweets around Maria's head:
From the blessings they bestow,
Our times are dated, and our eras move:
They govern and enlighten all below,
As thou dost all above.

Let our hero in the war
Active and fierce, like thee, appear:
Like thee, great son of Jove, like thee,
When clad in rising majesty,

Thou marchest down o'er Delos' hills confest,
With all thy arrows arm'd, in all thy glory drest.
Like thee, the hero does his arms employ,
The raging Python to destroy,
And give the injur'd nations peace and joy.

From fairest years, and Time's more happy stores,
Gather all the smiling hours;
Such as with friendly care have guarded
Patriots and kings in rightful wars;
Such as with conquest have rewarded
Triumphant victors' happy cares:
Such as story has recorded
Sacred to Nassau's long renown,
For countries sav'd, and battles won.

March them again in fair array,
And bid them form the happy day,
The happy day design'd to wait
On William's fame, and Europe's fate.
Let the happy day be crown'd
With great event, and fair success;
No brighter in the year be found,
But that which brings the victor home in peace.

Again thy godhead we implore,
Great in wisdom as in power;
Again, for good Maria's sake, and ours,
Choose out other smiling hours;
Such as with joyous wings have fled,
When happy counsels were advising;

Such as have lucky omens shed
O'er forming laws, and empires rising;
Such as many courses ran,
Hand in hand, a goodly train,
To bless the great Eliza's reign;
And in the typic glory show,
What fuller bliss Maria shall bestow.

As the solemn hours advance,
Mingled send into the dance
Many fraught with all the treasures,
Which thy eastern travel views;
Many wing'd with all the pleasures,
Man can ask, or Heav'n diffuse:
That great Maria all those joys may know,
Which, from her cares, upon her subjects flow.

For thy own glory sing our sov'reign's praise,
God of verses and of days:
Let all thy tuneful sons adorn
Their lasting work with William's name;
Let chosen Muses yet unborn
Take great Maria for their future theme:
Eternal structures let them raise,
On William's and Maria's praise:
Nor want new subject for the song,
Nor fear they can exhaust the store,
Till Nature's music lies unstrung,
Till thou, great God, shalt lose thy double pow'r,
And touch thy lyre, and shoot thy beams no more.

THE LADY'S LOOKING-GLASS.[1]

IN IMITATION OF A GREEK IDYLLIUM.

Celia and I the other day
Walk'd o'er the sand-hills to the sea:
The setting sun adorn'd the coast,
His beams entire, his fierceness lost:
And on the surface of the deep,
The winds lay only not asleep:
The nymph did like the scene appear,
Serenely pleasant, calmly fair:
Soft fell her words, as flew the air.
With secret joy I heard her say,
That she would never miss one day
A walk so fine, a sight so gay.
  But, oh the change! the winds grow high;
Impending tempests charge the sky;

[1] See Longinus's comparison of the Odyssey to the Setting Sun. Ed. Pearce, 8vo. p. 56.

"Whether Prior had the latter words in view, one cannot say; but it is difficult to conceive how the same image could be more accurately or forcibly transferred from one language to another. That lively and most agreeable writer was very fond of copying from the Grecian school, but always in such a manner as to show the master, where he even meant to imitate, of which this little poem is a beautiful instance: the learned will easily trace in the Looking-Glass of Prior the Poet and his Muse (as it may be inscribed) of Moschus. Caprice is the general subject of both poems, and many images of the latter are transplanted into the former." Note to Eunomus, 1774, vol. iv. p. 108.

The lightning flies; the thunder roars;
And big waves lash the frighten'd shores.
Struck with the horror of the sight,
She turns her head, and wings her flight;
And trembling vows, she'll ne'er again
Approach the shore, or view the main.
Once more at least look back, said I;
Thyself in that large glass descry:
When thou art in good-humour drest;
When gentle reason rules thy breast;
The sun upon the calmest sea
Appears not half so bright as thee:
'Tis then, that with delight I rove
Upon the boundless depth of love:
I bless my chain; I hand my oar;
Nor think on all I left on shore.
But when vain doubt, and groundless fear
Do that dear foolish bosom tear;
When the big lip, and wat'ry eye
Tell me, the rising storm is nigh:
'Tis then, thou art yon angry main,
Deform'd by winds, and dash'd by rain;
And the poor sailor, that must try
Its fury, labours less than I.
Shipwreck'd, in vain to land I make;
While Love and Fate still drive me back:
Forc'd to dote on thee thy own way,
I chide thee first, and then obey.
Wretched when from thee, vex'd when nigh,
I with thee, or without thee, die.

LOVE AND FRIENDSHIP:

A PASTORAL. BY MRS. ELIZABETH SINGER.[1]

AMARYLLIS.

While from the skies the ruddy sun descends,
And rising night the ev'ning shade extends;
While pearly dews o'erspread the fruitful field,
And closing flowers reviving odors yield;
Let us, beneath these spreading trees, recite
What from our hearts our Muses may indite.
Nor need we, in this close retirement, fear,
Lest any swain our am'rous secrets hear.

SILVIA.

To ev'ry shepherd I would mine proclaim:
Since fair Aminta is my softest theme:
A stranger to the loose delights of love,
My thoughts the nobler warmth of friendship prove:
And, while its pure and sacred fire I sing,
Chaste goddess of the groves, thy succour bring.

AMARYLLIS.

Propitious God of Love, my breast inspire
With all thy charms, with all thy pleasing fire:
Propitious God of Love, thy succour bring;
Whilst I thy darling, thy Alexis sing;
Alexis, as the opening blossoms fair,

[1] Afterwards the celebrated Mrs. Elizabeth Rowe. It is said Mr. Prior once made his addresses to this lady.

Lovely as light, and soft as yielding air.
For him each virgin sighs; and on the plains
The happy youth above each rival reigns.
Nor to the echoing groves, and whisp'ring spring,
In sweeter strains does artful Conon sing;
When loud applauses fill the crowded groves,
And Phœbus the superior song approves.

SILVIA.

Beauteous Aminta is as early light,
Breaking the melancholy shades of night.
When she is near, all anxious trouble flies;
And our reviving hearts confess her eyes.
Young love, and blooming joy, and gay desires,
In ev'ry breast the beauteous nymph inspires:
And on the plain when she no more appears,
The plain a dark and gloomy prospect wears.
In vain the streams roll on: the eastern breeze
Dances in vain among the trembling trees.
In vain the birds begin their ev'ning song,
And to the silent night their notes prolong:
Nor groves, nor crystal streams, nor verdant field
Does wonted pleasure in her absence yield.

AMARYLLIS.

And in his absence, all the pensive day,
In some obscure retreat I lonely stray;
All day to the repeating caves complain,
In mournful accents, and a dying strain.
Dear lovely youth, I cry to all around:
Dear lovely youth, the flattering vales resound.

SILVIA.

On flow'ry banks, by ev'ry murm'ring stream,
Aminta is my Muse's softest theme:
'Tis she that does my artful notes refine:
With fair Aminta's name my noblest verse shall
shine.

AMARYLLIS.

I'll twine fresh garlands for Alexis' brows,
And consecrate to him eternal vows:
The charming youth shall my Apollo prove:
He shall adorn my songs, and tune my voice to love.

TO THE AUTHOR OF THE FOREGOING PASTORAL

By Silvia if thy charming self be meant;
If friendship be thy virgin vows' extent;
O! let me in Aminta's praises join:
Hers my esteem shall be, my passion thine.
When for thy head the garland I prepare,
A second wreath shall bind Aminta's hair:
And when my choicest songs thy worth proclaim,
Alternate verse shall bless Aminta's name;
My heart shall own the justice of her cause,
And Love himself submit to Friendship's laws.
But, if beneath thy numbers' soft disguise,
Some favour'd swain, some true Alexis lies;
If Amaryllis breathes thy secret pains,

And thy fond heart beats measure to thy strains,
Mayst thou, howe'er I grieve, for ever find
The flame propitious, and the lover kind:
May Venus long exert her happy power,
And make thy beauty, like thy verse, endure;
May ev'ry god his friendly aid afford,
Pan guard thy flock, and Ceres bless thy board.
But, if by chance the series of thy joys
Permit one thought less cheerful to arise,
Piteous transfer it to the mournful swain,
Who loving much, who not belov'd again,
Feels an ill-fated passion's last excess,
And dies in woe, that thou mayst live in peace.

TO A LADY:

SHE REFUSING TO CONTINUE A DISPUTE WITH ME, AND LEAVING ME IN THE ARGUMENT.

AN ODE.

SPARE, gen'rous Victor, spare the slave,
Who did unequal war pursue;
That more than triumph he might have,
In being overcome by you.

In the dispute whate'er I said,
My heart was by my tongue belied;
And in my looks you might have read
How much I argu'd on your side.

You, far from danger as from fear,
  Might have sustain'd an open fight:
For seldom your opinions err;
  Your eyes are always in the right.

Why, fair one, would you not rely
  On Reason's force with Beauty's join'd?
Could I their prevalence deny,
  I must at once be deaf and blind.

Alas! not hoping to subdue,
  I only to the fight aspir'd:
To keep the beauteous foe in view
  Was all the glory I desir'd.

But she, howe'er of vict'ry sure,
  Contemns the wreath too long delay'd;
And, arm'd with more immediate power,
  Calls cruel silence to her aid.

Deeper to wound, she shuns the fight;
  She drops her arms, to gain the field;
Secures her conquest by her flight,
  And triumphs, when she seems to yield.

So when the Parthian turn'd his steed,
  And from the hostile camp withdrew,
With cruel skill the backward reed
  He sent; and as he fled, he slew.

SEEING THE DUKE OF ORMOND'S[1] PICTURE

AT SIR GODFREY KNELLER'S.

OUT from the injur'd canvas, Kneller, strike
These lines too faint: the picture is not like.
Exalt thy thought, and try thy toil again:
Dreadful in arms, on Landen's[2] glorious plain

1 James Duke of Ormond, eldest son of Thomas, Earl of Ossory. He succeeded his grandfather in title and estate in the year 1688; was bred at Christ Church in the University of Oxford, and after holding many considerable posts during the reigns of King William and Queen Anne, was, in the beginning of the reign of George the First, attainted of high treason on account of his being concerned in the unpopular measures of the last four years of Queen Anne's reign. He died in exile in the year 1745, in a very advanced age.

2 At the battle of Landen the Duke of Ormond was taken prisoner after his horse was shot under him, and he had received many wounds. Mr. Dryden, in his dedication prefixed to his Fables in the year 1699, says, "Yet not to be wholly silent of all your charities, I must stay a little on one action, which preferred the relief of others to the consideration of yourself. When, in the battle of Landen, your heat of courage (a fault only pardonable to your youth) had transported you so far before your friends, that they were unable to follow, much less to succour you; when you were not only dangerously, but in all appearance mortally wounded, when in that desperate condition you were made prisoner, and carried to Namur, at that time in possession of the French; then it was, my Lord, that you took a considerable part of what was remitted to you of your own revenues, and

Place Ormond's duke: impendent in the air
Let his keen sabre, comet-like, appear,
Where'er it points, denouncing death: below
Draw routed squadrons, and the num'rous foe
Falling beneath, or flying from his blow:
Till weak with wounds, and cover'd o'er with blood,
Which from the patriot's breast in torrents flow'd,
He faints: his steed no longer feels the rein;

as a memorable instance of your heroic charity, put it into the hands of Count Guiscard, who was Governor of the place, to be distributed among your fellow-prisoners. The French commander, charmed with the greatness of your soul, accordingly consigned it to the use for which it was intended by the donor: by which means the lives of so many miserable men were saved, and a comfortable provision made for their subsistence, who had otherwise perished, had not you been the companion of their misfortune: or rather sent by Providence, like another Joseph, to keep out famine from invading those, whom in humility you called your brethren. How happy was it for those poor creatures, that your grace was made their fellow-sufferer! and how glorious for you, that you chose to want, rather than not relieve the wants of others! The heathen poet, in commending the charity of Dido to the Trojans, spoke like a Christian: *Non ignara mali, miseris succurrere disco.* All men, even those of a different interest, and contrary principles, must praise this action, as the most eminent for piety, not only in this degenerate age, but almost in any of the former; when men were made *de meliore luto;* when examples of charity were frequent, and when they were in being, *Teucri pulcherrima proles, magnanimi heroes nati melioribus annis.* No envy can detract from this; it will shine in history; and, like swans, grow whiter the longer it endures: and the name of Ormond will be more celebrated in his captivity, than in his greatest triumphs."

But stumbles o'er the heap his hand had slain.
And now exhausted, bleeding, pale he lies;
Lovely, sad object! in his half-clos'd eyes
Stern vengeance yet, and hostile terror stand:
His front yet threatens; and his frowns command:
The Gallic chiefs their troops around him call;
Fear to approach him, though they see him fall.
  O Kneller, could thy shades and lights express
The perfect hero in that glorious dress;
Ages to come might Ormond's picture know;
And palms for thee beneath his laurels grow:
In spite of Time thy work might ever shine;
Nor Homer's colours last so long as thine.

CELIA TO DAMON.

Atque in amore mala hæc proprio, summeque secundo
Inveniuntur— LUCRET. lib. iv.

What can I say, what arguments can prove
My truth, what colours can describe my love;
If its excess and fury be not known,
In what thy Celia has already done?
  Thy infant flames, whilst yet they were conceal'd
In tim'rous doubts, with pity I beheld;
With easy smiles dispell'd the silent fear,
That durst not tell me what I died to hear:
In vain I strove to check my growing flame,

Or shelter passion under friendship's name:
You saw my heart, how it my tongue belied;
And when you press'd, how faintly I denied—
  Ere guardian thought could bring its scatter'd aid;
Ere reason could support the doubting maid;
My soul surpris'd, and from herself disjoin'd,
Left all reserve, and all the sex behind:
From your command her motions she receiv'd;
And not for me, but you, she breath'd and liv'd.
  But ever blest be Cytherea's shrine,
And fires eternal on her altars shine;
Since thy dear breast has felt an equal wound;
Since in thy kindness my desires are crown'd,
By thy each look, and thought, and care, 'tis shown,
Thy joys are centred all in me alone;
And sure I am, thou wouldst not change this hour
For all the white ones Fate has in its power.—
  Yet thus belov'd, thus loving to excess,
Yet thus receiving and returning bliss,
In this great moment, in this golden now,
When every trace of what, or when, or how
Should from my soul by raging love be torn,
And far on swelling seas of rapture borne;
A melancholy tear afflicts my eye;
And my heart labours with a sudden sigh:
Invading fears repel my coward joy,
And ills foreseen the present bliss destroy.
  Poor as it is, this Beauty was the cause,
That with first sighs your panting bosom rose:

But with no owner Beauty long will stay,
Upon the wings of Time borne swift away:
Pass but some fleeting years, and these poor eyes
(Where now without a boast some lustre lies)
No longer shall their little honours keep;
Shall only be of use to read, or weep:
And on this forehead, where your verse has said,
The Loves delighted, and the Graces play'd,
Insulting Age will trace his cruel way,
And leave sad marks of his destructive sway.
Mov'd by my charms, with them your love may cease,
And as the fuel sinks, the flame decrease:
Or angry Heav'n may quicker darts prepare,
And Sickness strike what Time awhile would spare.
Then will my swain his glowing vows renew;
Then will his throbbing heart to mine beat true;
When my own face deters me from my glass;
And Kneller only shows what Celia was.
Fantastic fame may sound her wild alarms:
Your country, as you think, may want your arms.
You may neglect, or quench, or hate the flame,
Whose smoke too long obscur'd your rising name:
And quickly cold indiff'rence will ensue;
When you Love's joys through Honour's optic view.
Then Celia's loudest prayer will prove too weak,
To this abandon'd breast to bring you back;
When my lost lover the tall ship ascends,
With music gay, and wet with jovial friends:
The tender accents of a woman's cry

Will pass unheard, will unregarded die;
When the rough seaman's louder shouts prevail;
When fair occasion shows the springing gale;
And Int'rest guides the helm; and Honours swells the sail.

Some wretched lines from this neglected hand
May find my hero on the foreign strand,
Warm with new fires, and pleas'd with new command:
While she who wrote 'em, of all joy bereft,
To the rude censure of the world is left;
Her mangled fame in barb'rous pastime lost,
The coxcomb's novel, and the drunkard's toast.

But nearer care (O pardon it!) supplies
Sighs to my breast, and sorrow to my eyes.
Love, Love himself (the only friend I have)
May scorn his triumph, having bound his slave.
That tyrant god, that restless conqueror
May quit his pleasure, to assert his pow'r;
Forsake the provinces that bless his sway,
To vanquish those which will not yet obey.

Another nymph with fatal power may rise,
To damp the sinking beams of Celia's eyes;
With haughty pride may hear her charms confest,
And scorn the ardent vows that I have blest:
You ev'ry night may sigh for her in vain,
And rise each morning to some fresh disdain;
While Celia's softest look may cease to charm,
And her embraces want the power to warm:
While these fond arms, thus circling you, may prove

More heavy chains than those of hopeless love.
Just gods! all other things their like produce:
The vine arises from her mother's juice:
When feeble plants, or tender flowers decay,
They to their seed their images convey:
Where the old myrtle her good influence sheds,
Sprigs of like leaf erect their filial heads:
And when the parent-rose decays and dies,
With a resembling face the daughter-buds arise.
That product only which our passions bear,
Eludes the planter's miserable care:
While blooming Love assures us golden fruit,
Some inborn poison taints the secret root:
Soon fall the flowers of joy; soon seeds of hatred shoot.
Say, shepherd, say, are these reflections true?
Or was it but the woman's fear, that drew
This cruel scene, unjust to Love and you?
Will you be only, and for ever mine?
Shall neither time, nor age our souls disjoin?
From this dear bosom shall I ne'er be torn?
Or you grow cold, respectful, and forsworn?
And can you not for her you love do more
Than any youth for any nymph before?

AN ODE

PRESENTED TO THE KING, ON HIS MAJESTY'S ARRIVAL IN HOLLAND, AFTER THE QUEEN'S DEATH. MDCXCV.[1]

Quis desiderio sit pudor aut modus
Tam cari capitis? Præcipe lugubres
Cantus, Melpomene.

At Mary's tomb, (sad, sacred place!)
The virtues shall their vigils keep:
And every muse, and every grace
In solemn state shall ever weep.

The future, pious, mournful fair,
Oft as the rolling years return,
With fragrant wreaths, and flowing hair,
Shall visit her distinguish'd urn.

For her the wise and great shall mourn;
When late records her deeds repeat:
Ages to come, and men unborn
Shall bless her name, and sigh her fate.

Fair Albion shall, with faithful trust,
Her holy Queen's sad reliques guard,
Till Heav'n awakes the precious dust,
And gives the saint her full reward.

1 Queen Mary died on the 28th December, 1694, in the 33d year of her age.

But let the king dismiss his woes,
  Reflecting on his fair renown;
And take the cypress from his brows,
  To put his wonted laurels on.

If press'd by grief our monarch stoops;
  In vain the British lions roar:
If he, whose hand sustain'd them, droops,
  The Belgic darts will wound no more.

Embattled princes wait the chief,
  Whose voice should rule, whose arm should lead;
And, in kind murmurs, chide that grief,
  Which hinders Europe being freed.

The great example they demand,
  Who still to conquest led the way;
Wishing him present to command,
  As they stand ready to obey.

They seek that joy, which used to glow,
  Expanded on the hero's face;
When the thick squadrons press'd the foe,
  And William led the glorious chace.

To give the mourning nations joy,
  Restore them thy auspicious light,
Great sun: with radiant beams destroy
  Those clouds, which keep thee from our sight.

Let thy sublime meridian course
  For Mary's setting rays atone;
Our lustre with redoubled force
  Must now proceed from thee alone.

See, pious King, with diff'rent strife
  Thy struggling Albion's bosom torn:
So much she fears for William's life,
  That Mary's fate she dares not mourn.

Her beauty, in thy softer half
  Buried and lost, she ought to grieve:
But let her strength in thee be safe:
  And let her weep; but let her live.

Thou, guardian angel, save the land
  From thy own grief, her fiercest foe:
Lest Britain, rescued by thy hand,
  Should bend and sink beneath thy woe.

Her former triumphs all are vain,
  Unless new trophies still be sought,
And hoary majesty sustain
  The battles, which thy youth has fought.

Where now is all that fearful love,
  Which made her hate the war's alarms?
That soft excess, with which she strove
  To keep her hero in her arms?

While still she chid the coming spring,
  Which call'd him o'er his subject seas:
While, for the safety of the king,
  She wish'd the victor's glory less.

'Tis chang'd; 'tis gone: sad Britain now
  Hastens her lord to foreign wars:
Happy, if toils may break his woe,
  Or danger may divert his cares.

In martial din she drowns her sighs,
  Lest he the rising grief should hear;
She pulls her helmet o'er her eyes,
  Lest he should see the falling tear.

Go, mighty prince, let France be taught,
  How constant minds by grief are tried;
How great the land, that wept and fought,
  When William led, and Mary died.

Fierce in the battle make it known,
  Where death with all his darts is seen,
That he can touch thy heart with none,
  But that which struck the beauteous queen.

Belgia indulg'd her open grief,
  While yet her master was not near;
With sullen pride refus'd relief,
  And sat obdurate in despair.

As waters from their sluices, flow'd
  Unbounded sorrow from her eyes:
To earth her bended front she bow'd,
  And sent her wailings to the skies.

But when her anxious lord return'd,
  Rais'd is her head, her eyes are dried;
She smiles, as William ne'er had mourn'd;
  She looks, as Mary ne'er had died.

That freedom which all sorrows claim,
  She does for thy content resign:
Her piety itself would blame,
  If her regrets should waken thine.

To cure thy woe, she shows thy fame;
  Lest the great mourner should forget,
That all the race, whence Orange came,
  Made Virtue triumph over Fate.

William his country's cause could fight,
  And with his blood her freedom seal:
Maurice and Henry guard that right,
  For which their pious parents fell.

How heroes rise, how patriots set,
  Thy father's bloom and death may tell:
Excelling others these were great:
  Thou, greater still, must these excel.

The last fair instance thou must give,
 Whence Nassau's virtue can be tried;
And shew the world, that thou canst live,
 Intrepid, as thy consort died.

Thy virtue, whose resistless force
 No dire event could ever stay,
Must carry on its destin'd course,
 Though Death and Envy stop the way.

For Britain's sake, for Belgia's, live:
 Pierc'd by their grief forget thy own:
New toils endure; new conquest give;
 And bring them ease, though thou hast none.

Vanquish again; though she be gone,
 Whose garland crown'd the victor's hair;
And reign, though she has left the throne,
 Who made thy glory worth thy care.

Fair Britain never yet before
 Breath'd to her king a useless pray'r:
Fond Belgia never did implore,
 While William turn'd averse his ear.

But should the weeping hero now
 Relentless to their wishes prove;
Should he recall, with pleasing woe,
 The object of his grief and love;

Her face with thousand beauties blest,
  Her mind with thousand virtues stor'd,
Her power with boundless joy confest,
  Her person only not ador'd:

Yet ought his sorrow to be check'd;
  Yet ought his passions to abate:
If the great mourner would reflect,
  Her glory in her death complete.

She was instructed to command,
  Great king, by long obeying thee:
Her sceptre, guided by thy hand,
  Preserv'd the isles, and rul'd the sea.

But oh! 'twas little, that her life
  O'er earth and water bears thy fame:
In death, 'twas worthy William's wife,
  Amidst the stars to fix his name.

Beyond where matter moves, or place
  Receives its forms, thy virtues roll:
From Mary's glory, angels trace
  The beauty of her partner's soul.

Wise Fate, which does its Heav'n decree
  To heroes, when they yield their breath
Hastens thy triumph. Half of thee
  Is deified before thy death.

Alone to thy renown 'tis giv'n,
Unbounded through all worlds to go:
While she, great saint, rejoices Heav'n;
And thou sustain'st the orb below.

IN IMITATION OF ANACREON.

Let 'em censure: what care I?
The herd of critics I defy.
Let the wretches know, I write,
Regardless of their grace, or spite.
No, no: the fair, the gay, the young
Govern the numbers of my song.
All that they approve is sweet,
And all is sense that they repeat.
Bid the warbling Nine retire:
Venus, string thy servant's lyre:
Love shall be my endless theme:
Pleasure shall triumph over Fame:
And when these maxims I decline,
Apollo, may thy fate be mine:
May I grasp at empty praise;
And lose the nymph, to gain the bays.

AN ODE.

THE merchant, to secure his treasure,
  Conveys it in a borrow'd name:
Euphelia serves to grace my measure;
  But Cloe is my real flame.

My softest verse, my darling lyre,
  Upon Euphelia's toilet lay;
When Cloe noted her desire,
  That I should sing, that I should play.

My lyre I tune, my voice I raise;
  But with my numbers mix my sighs:
And whilst I sing Euphelia's praise,
  I fix my soul on Cloe's eyes.

Fair Cloe blush'd: Euphelia frown'd:
  I sung and gaz'd: I play'd and trembled
And Venus to the Loves around
  Remark'd, how ill we all dissembled.

ODE SUR LA PRISE DE NAMUR,

PAR LES ARMES DU ROY, L'ANNEE MDCXCII. PAR MONSIEUR BOILEAU DESPREAUX.

AN ENGLISH BALLAD,

ON THE TAKING OF NAMUR, BY THE KING OF GREAT BRITAIN, MDCXCV.

ODE

SUR LA PRISE DE NAMUR, PAR LES ARMES DU ROY, L'ANNEE MDCXCII. PAR MONSIEUR BOILEAU DESPREAUX.

QUELLE docte et sainte yvresse
Aujourd'huy me fait la loy?
Chastes nymphes du Permesse,
N'est-ce pas vous que je voy?
Accourez, troupe sçavante:
Des sons que ma lyre enfante
Ces arbres sont réjoüis:
Marquez en bien la cadence:
Et vous, vents, faites silence:
Je vais parler de Louis.

Dans ses chansons immortelles,
Comme un aigle audacieux,
Pindare étendant ses aisles,
Fuit loin des vulgaires yeux.
Mais, ô ma fidèle lyre,
Si, dans l'ardeur qui m'inspire,
Tu peux suivre mes transports;
Les chesnes des monts de Thrace
N'ont rien oüi, que n'efface
La douceur de tes accords.

AN ENGLISH BALLAD

ON THE TAKING OF NAMUR BY THE KING OF GREAT BRITAIN, MDCXCV.

Dulce est desipere in loco.[1]

Some folks are drunk, yet do not know it:
  So might not Bacchus give you law?
Was it a Muse, O lofty Poet,
  Or virgin of St. Cyr, you saw?
Why all this fury? What's the matter,
  That oaks must come from Thrace to dance?
Must stupid stocks be taught to flatter?
  And is there no such wood in France?
Why must the winds all hold their tongue?
  If they a little breath should raise,
Would that have spoil'd the Poet's song,
  Or puff'd away the monarch's praise?

Pindar, that eagle, mounts the skies:
  While Virtue leads the noble way:
Too like a vulture Boileau flies,
  Where sordid Int'rest shows the prey.
When once the Poet's honour ceases,
  From reason far his transports rove
And Boileau, for eight hundred pieces,
  Makes Louis take the wall of Jove.

[1] This ballad received great alterations after the first edition of it. The taking of Namur by the French in the year

Est-ce Apollon et Neptune,
Qui sur ces rocs sourcilleux
Ont, compagnons de fortune,
Basti ces murs orgueilleux?
De leur enceinte fameuse
La Sambre unie à la Meuse,
Défend le fatal abord;
Et par cent bouches horribles
L'airain sur ces monts terribles
Vomit le fer, et la mort.

Dix mille vaillans Alcides
Les bordant de toutes parts,
D'éclairs au loin homicides
Font petiller, leurs remparts:
Et dans sons sein infidèle
Par toute la terre y recèle
Un feu prest à s'élancer,
Qui soudain perçant son goufre,
Ouvre un sépulchre de soufre,
A quiconque ose avancer.

Namur, devant tes murailles
Jadis la Grèce eust vingt ans

1692, and the retaking it by the English in the year 1695, were considered by each nation as events which contributed to raise the honour and reputation of the respective kingdoms. Both sieges were carried on by the rival monarchs in person, and the success of each was celebrated by the best writers of the times. It may be doubted whether there ever was a burlesque more agreeably or happily executed than this by our excellent countryman.

Neptune and Sol came from above,
Shap'd like Megrigny and the Vauban:[1]
They arm'd these rocks: then show'd old Jove
Of Marli wood the wondrous plan.
Such walls, these three wise gods agreed,
By human force could ne'er be shaken:
But you and I in Homer read
Of gods, as well as men, mistaken.
Sambre and Maese their waves may join;
But ne'er can William's force restrain:
He'll pass them both, who pass'd the Boyne:[2]
Remember this and arm the Seine.

Full fifteen thousand lusty fellows
With fire and sword the fort maintain;
Each was a Hercules, you tell us,
Yet out they march'd like common men.
Cannons above, and mines below,
Did death and tombs for foes contrive:
Yet matters have been order'd so,
That most of us are still alive.

If Namur be compar'd to Troy;
Then Britain's boys excell'd the Greeks:

[1] Two celebrated engineers.

[2] In the year 1690, notwithstanding numberless difficulties, this famous passage of the river brought on a general engagement, which entirely destroyed the power of King James, and put an end to every hope of success, which he had before entertained from his expedition to Ireland.

Sans fruit veu les funérailles
De ses plus fiers combattans.
Quelle effroyable Puissance
Aujourd'huy pourtant s'avance,
Preste à foudroyer tes monts ?
Quel bruit, quel feu l'environne ?
C'est Jupiter en personne ;
Ou c'est le vainqueur de Mons.

N'en doute point : c'est luy-mesme.
Tout brille en luy ; tout est roy.
Dans Bruxelles Nassau blême
Commence à trembler pour toy.
En vain il voit le Batâve,
Desormais docile Esclâve,
Rangé sous ses étendars :
En vain au Lion Belgique
Il voit l'aigle Germanique
Uni sous les léopards.

Plein de la frayeur nouvelle,
Dont ses sens sont agités,
A son secours il appelle
Les peuples les plus vantéz.

Their siege did ten long years employ;
  We've done our bus'ness in ten weeks.
What godhead does so fast advance,
  With dreadful power those hills to gain?
'Tis little Will, the scourge of France;
  No godhead, but the first of men.
His mortal arm exerts the power
  To keep ev'n Mons's victor under:[1]
And that same Jupiter no more
  Shall fright the world with impious thunder.

Our king thus trembles at Namur,
  Whilst Villeroy, who ne'er afraid is,[2]
To Bruxelles marches on secure,
  To bomb the monks and scare the ladies.
After this glorious expedition,
  One battle makes the marshal great:
He must perform the king's commission:
  Who knows, but Orange may retreat?
Kings are allow'd to feign the gout,
  Or be prevail'd with not to fight:
And mighty Louis hop'd, no doubt,
  That William would preserve that right.

From Seine and Loire, to Rhone and Po,
  See ev'ry mother's son appear:
In such a case ne'er blame a foe,
  If he betrays some little fear.

1 Mons surrendered to Louis XIV. 10th April, 1691.

2 While King William was carrying on the siege of Na-

Ceux là viennent du rivage,
Où s'enorgueillit le Tage
De l'or, qui roule en ses eaux;
Ceux-ci des champs, où la neige
Des marais de la Norvège
Neuf mois couvre les roseaux.

Mais qui fait enfler la Sambre?
Sous les Jumeaux effrayéz,
Des froids torrens de Decembre
Les champs par tout sont noyéz.
Cérès s'enfuit, éplorée
De voir en proye à Borée
Ses guerets d'epics chargéz,
Et sous les urns fangeuses
Des Hyades orageuses
Tous ses trésors submergéz.

Déployez toutes vos rages,
Princes, vents, peuples, frimats;
Ramassez tous vos nuages;
Rassemblez tous vos soldats.
Malgré vous Namur en poudre
S'en va tomber sous la foudre

mur, Marshal Villeroy, in order to compel him to relinquish that design, marched to Brussels and bombarded that town.

He comes, the mighty Villeroy comes;
  Finds a small river in his way;
So waves his colours, beats his drums,
  And thinks it prudent there to stay.
The Gallic troops breathe blood and war;
  The Marshal cares not to march faster;
Poor Villeroy moves so slowly here,
  We fancied all, it was his master.

Will no kind flood, no friendly rain
  Disguise the marshal's plain disgrace:
No torrents swell the low Mehayne?
  The world will say, he durst not pass.
Why will no Hyades appear,
  Dear Poet, on the banks of Sambrè?
Just as they did that mighty year,
  When you turn'd June into December.
The water-nymphs are too unkind
  To Villeroy; are the land-nymphs so?
And fly they all, at once combin'd
  To shame a general, and a beau?

Truth, Justice, Sense, Religion, Fame,
  May join to finish William's story:
Nations set free may bless his name;
  And France in secret own his glory.
But Ypres, Maestricht, and Cambray,
  Besançon, Ghent, St. Omers, Lisle,
Courtray, and Dole—ye critics, say,
  How poor to this was Pindar's style!

Qui domta Lille, Courtray,
Grand la superbe Espagnole,
Saint Omer, Bezançon, Dole,
Ypres, Mastricht, et Cambray.

Mes présages s'accomplissent :
Il commence à chanceler :
Sous les coups qui retentissent
Ses murs s'en vont s'écrouler.
Mars en feu qui les domine,
Souffle à grand bruit leur ruine,
Et les bombes dans les airs
Allant chercher le tonnerre
Semblent tombant sur la terre,
Vouloir s'ouvrir les enfers.

Accourez, Nassau, Bavière,
De ces murs l'unique espoir :
A couvert d'une rivière
Venez : vous pouvez tout voir.
Considérez ces approches :
Voyez grimper sur ces roches
Ces athletes belliqueux ;
Et dans les eaux, dans la flame,
Louis à tout donnant l'âme,
Marcher, courir, avec eux.

With ekes and alsos tack thy strain,
  Great bard; and sing the deathless prince,
Who lost Namur the same campaign,
  He bought Dixmuyd, and plunder'd Deynse.

I'll hold ten pound my dream is out:
  I'd tell it you, but for the rattle
Of those confounded drums; no doubt
  Yon bloody rogues intend a battle.
Dear me! a hundred thousand French
  With terror fill the neighb'ring field:
While William carries on the trench,
  Till both the town and castle yield.
Villeroy to Boufflers should advance,
  Says Mars, through cannons' mouths in fire;
Id est, one mareschal of France
  Tells t'other, he can come no nigher.

Regain the lines the shortest way,
  Villeroy; or to Versailles take post;
For, having seen it, thou canst say
  The steps, by which Namur was lost.
The smoke and flame may vex thy sight:
  Look not once back: but as thou goest,
Quicken the squadrons in their flight,
  And bid the d—l take the slowest.
Think not what reason to produce,
  From Louis to conceal thy fear:
He'll own the strength of thy excuse;
  Tell him that William was but there.

Contemplez dans la tempeste,
Qui sort de ces boulevars,
La plume qui sur sa teste
Attire tous les regards.
A cet astre redoubtable
Toujours un sort favorable
S'attache dans les combats :
Et toujours avec la gloire
Mars amenant la Victoire
Vole, et le suit à grands pas.

Grands défenseurs de l'Espagne,
Montrez-vous : il en est temps :
Courage ; vers la Mahagne
Voilà vos drapeaux flottans.
Jamais ses ondes craintives
N'ont veû sur leurs foibles rives
Tant de guerriers s'amasser.
Courez donc : qui vous retarde ?
Tout l'univers vous regarde.
N'osez-vous la traverser ?

Loin de fermer le passage
A vos nombreux bataillons,
Luxembourg a du rivage
Reculé ses pavillons.
Quoy ? leur seul aspect vous glace ?
Où sont ces chefs pleins d'audace,
Jadis si prompts à marcher,
Qui devoient de la Tamise,
Et de la Drâve soûmise,
Jusqu'à Paris nous chercher ?

Now let us look for Louis' feather,
  That us'd to shine so like a star:
The gen'rals could not get together,
  Wanting that influence, great in war.
O Poet! thou hadst been discreeter,
  Hanging the monarch's hat so high;
If thou hadst dubb'd thy star a meteor,
  That did but blaze, and rove, and die.

To animate the doubtful fight,
  Namur in vain expects that ray:
In vain France hopes, the sickly light
  Should shine near William's fuller day:
It knows Versailles, its proper station;
  Nor cares for any foreign sphere:
Where you see Boileau's constellation,
  Be sure no danger can be near.

The French had gather'd all their force;
  And William met them in their way:
Yet off they brush'd, both foot and horse.
  What has friend Boileau left to say?
When his high Muse is bent upon't,
  To sing her king—that great commander,
Or on the shores of Hellespont,
  Or in the valleys near Scamander;
Would it not spoil his noble task,
  If any foolish Phrygian there is
Impertinent enough to ask,
  How far Namur may be from Paris.

Cependant l'effroy redouble
Sur les remparts de Namur ;
Son gouverneur qui se trouble
S'enfuit sous son dernier mur.
Déjà jusques à ses portes
Je voy monter nos cohortes,
La flame et le fer en main :
Et sur les monceaux de piques,
De corps morts, de rocs, de briques,
S'ouvrir un large chemin.

C'en est fait. Je viens d'entendre
Sur ces rochers éperdus
Battre un signal pour se rendre :
Le feu cesse. Ils sont rendus.
Dépouillez votre arrogance,
Fiers ennemis de la France,
Et desormais gracieux,
Allez à Liege, à Bruxelles,
Porter les humbles nouvelles
De Namur pris à vos yeux.

Two stanzas more before we end,
  Of death, pikes, rocks, arms, bricks, and fire:
Leave them behind you, honest friend;
  And with your countrymen retire.
Your ode is spoilt; Namur is freed;
  For Dixmuyd something yet is due:
So good Count Guiscard may proceed;[1]
  But Boufflers, Sir, one word with you—

'Tis done. In sight of these commanders,
  Who neither fight, nor raise the siege,
The foes of France march safe through Flanders;
  Divide to Bruxelles, or to Liege.
Send, Fame, this news to Trianon,
  That Boufflers may new honours gain:
He the same play by land has shown,
  As Tourville did upon the main.[2]
Yet is the marshal made a peer!
  O William, may thy arms advance;
That he may lose Dinant next year,
  And so be constable of France.

[1] Count Guiscard was commander of the town of Namur. Marshal Bouffleurs of the castle there.

[2] M. de Tourville was commander of the French squadron which engaged Admiral Russell in 1692, off La Hogue.

PRESENTED TO THE KING,

AT HIS ARRIVAL IN HOLLAND, AFTER THE DISCOVERY OF THE CONSPIRACY,[1] MDCXCVI.

Serus in cœlum redeas; diuque
Lætus intersis populo Quirini:
Neve te nostris vitiis iniquum
Ocyor aura
Tollat—— HOR. ad Augustum.

YE careful angels, whom eternal Fate
Ordains, on earth and human acts to wait;
Who turn with secret power this restless ball,
And bid predestin'd empires rise and fall:
Your sacred aid religious monarchs own,
When first they merit, then ascend the throne:
But tyrants dread ye, lest your just decree
Transfer the power, and set the people free.
See rescu'd Britain at your altars bow;
And hear her hymns your happy care avow:
That still her axes and her rods support
The judge's frown, and grace the awful court;
That Law with all her pompous terror stands,
To wrest the dagger from the traitor's hands;
And rigid justice reads the fatal word,
Poises the balance first, then draws the sword.

1 This conspiracy is generally called the Assassination Plot. Sir John Fenwick was executed for being concerned in it.

Britain her safety to your guidance owns,
That she can sep'rate parricides from sons;
That, impious rage disarm'd, she lives and reigns,
Her freedom kept by him, who broke her chains.
And thou, great minister, above the rest
Of guardian spirits, be thou for ever blest;
Thou, who of old wert sent to Israel's court,
With secret aid great David's strong support;
To mock the frantic rage of cruel Saul,
And strike the useless javelin to the wall.
Thy later care o'er William's temples held,
On Boyne's propitious banks, the heav'nly shield;
When power divine did sovereign right declare,
And cannons mark'd whom they were bid to spare.
Still, blessed angel, be thy care the same!
Be William's life untouch'd, as is his fame!
Let him own thine, as Britain owns his hand:
Save thou the king, as he has sav'd the land!
We angels' forms in pious monarchs view;
We reverence William; for he acts like you;
Like you, commission'd to chastise and bless,
He must avenge the world, and give it peace.
Indulgent Fate our potent prayer receives;
And still Britannia smiles, and William lives.
The hero dear to earth, by heav'n belov'd,
By troubles must be vex'd, by dangers prov'd:
His foes must aid to make his fame complete,
And fix his throne secure on their defeat.
So, though with sudden rage the tempest comes;
Though the winds roar, and though the water foams,

Imperial Britain on the sea looks down,
And smiling sees her rebel subject frown:
Striking her cliff, the storm confirms her pow'r;
The waves but whiten her triumphant shore:
In vain they would advance, in vain retreat:
Broken they dash, and perish at her feet.
  For William still new wonders shall be shown:
The powers that rescued, shall preserve the throne.
Safe on his darling Britain's joyful sea,
Behold, the monarch ploughs his liquid way:
His fleets in thunder through the world declare,
Whose empire they obey, whose arms they bear.
Bless'd by aspiring winds, he finds the strand
Blacken'd with clouds; he sees the nations stand
Blessing his safety, proud of his command.
In various tongues he hears the captains dwell
On their great leader's praise; by turns they tell,
And listen, each with emulous glory fir'd,
How William conquer'd, and how France retir'd;
How Belgia, freed, the hero's arm confess'd,
But trembled for the courage which she bless'd.
  O Louis, from this great example know,
To be at once a hero and a foe:
By sounding trumpets, hear, and rattling drums,
When William to the open vengeance comes:
And see the soldier plead the monarch's right,
Heading his troops, and foremost in the fight.
  Hence then, close Ambush and perfidious War,
Down to your native seats of Night repair.
And thou, Bellona, weep thy cruel pride

Restrain'd, behind the victor's chariot tied
In brazen knots, and everlasting chains,
(So Europe's peace, so William's fate ordains).
While on the ivory chair, in happy state,
He sits, secure in innocence, and great
In regal clemency; and views beneath
Averted darts of rage, and pointless arms of death.

TO CLOE WEEPING.

See, whilst thou weep'st, fair Cloe, see
The world in sympathy with thee.
The cheerful birds no longer sing;
Each droops his head, and hangs his wing.
The clouds have bent their bosom lower,
And shed their sorrows in a shower.
The brooks beyond their limits flow;
And louder murmurs speak their woe.
The nymphs and swains adopt thy cares;
They heave thy sighs, and weep thy tears.
Fantastic nymph! that grief should move
Thy heart obdurate against Love.
Strange tears! whose power can soften all,
But that dear breast on which they fall.

TO MR. HOWARD.[1] AN ODE.

Dear Howard, from the soft assaults of Love,
Poets and painters never are secure;
Can I untouch'd the fair one's passions move?
Or thou draw beauty, and not feel its power?

[1] "Hugh Howard, better known by these beautiful verses to him, than by his own works, was son of Ralph Howard, doctor of physic, and was born in Dublin, February 7, 1675. His father being driven from Ireland by the troubles that followed the Revolution, brought the lad to England, who discovering a disposition to the arts and Belles Lettres, was sent to travel in 1697; and, in his way to Italy, passed through Holland in the train of Thomas, Earl of Pembroke, one of the plenipotentiaries at the treaty of Ryswick. Mr. Howard proceeded as he had intended, and having visited France and Italy, returned home in October, 1700.

"Some years he passed in Dublin: the greatest and latter part of his life he spent entirely in England, practising painting, at least with applause; but having ingratiated himself by his fame and knowledge of lands with men of the first rank, particularly the Duke of Devonshire and Lord Pembroke, and by a parsimonious management of his good fortune, and of what he received with his wife, he was enabled to quit the practical part of his profession for the last twenty years of his life; the former peer having obtained for him the posts of Keeper of the State Papers, and Paymaster of his Majesty's Palaces. In this pleasing situation he amused himself with forming a large collection of prints,

To great Apelles when young Ammon brought[1]
The darling idol of his captive heart;
And the pleas'd nymph with kind attention sat,
To have her charms recorded by his art:

The am'rous master own'd her potent eyes;
Sigh'd when he look'd, and trembled as he drew;
Each flowing line confirm'd his first surprise,
And as the piece advanc'd, the passion grew.

While Philip's son, while Venus' son was near,
What different tortures does his bosom feel!
Great was the rival, and the god severe:
Nor could he hide his flame, nor durst reveal.

The prince, renown'd in bounty as in arms,
With pity saw the ill-conceal'd distress;
Quitted his title to Campaspe's charms,
And gave the fair one to the friend's embrace.

books, and medals, which at his death * (March 27, 1737), he bequeathed to his only brother Robert Howard, Bishop of Elphin, who transported them to Ireland.

"Mr. Howard's picture was drawn by Dahl, very like, and published in mezzotinto about a year before his death. Howard himself etched from a drawing of Carlo Marati, a head of Padra Resta, the collector, with his spectacles on, turning over a large book of drawings."

[1] See Pliny's Natural History, B. 35. C. 10.

---

* He died in Pall-Mall, and was buried at Richmond. Walpole's Anecdotes, vol. iii. p. 156.

Thus the more beauteous Cloe sat to thee,
  Good Howard, emulous of the Grecian art:
But happy thou, from Cupid's arrow free,
  And flames that pierc'd thy predecessor's heart.

Had thy poor breast receiv'd an equal pain;
  Had I been vested with the monarch's power;
Thou must have sigh'd, unlucky youth, in vain;
  Nor from my bounty hadst thou found a cure.

Though to convince thee, that the friend did feel
  A kind concern for thy ill-fated care,
I would have sooth'd the flame I could not heal;
  Giv'n thee the world, though I withheld the fair.

LOVE DISARMED.

BENEATH a myrtle's verdant shade
As Cloe half asleep was laid,
Cupid perch'd lightly on her breast,
And in that heav'n desir'd to rest:
Over her paps his wings he spread:
Between he found a downy bed,
And nestled in his little head.
  Still lay the god: the nymph surpris'd,
Yet mistress of herself, devis'd
How she the vagrant might enthral,
And captive him, who captives all.

Her bodice half-way she unlac'd;
About his arms she slily cast
The silken bond, and held him fast.
The god awak'd; and thrice in vain
He strove to break the cruel chain;
And thrice in vain he shook his wing,
Incumber'd in the silken string.
Flutt'ring the god, and weeping said,
Pity poor Cupid, generous maid,
Who happen'd, being blind, to stray,
And on thy bosom lost his way;
Who stray'd, alas! but knew too well,
He never there must hope to dwell:
Set an unhappy pris'ner free,
Who ne'er intended harm to thee.
To me pertains not, she replies,
To know or care where Cupid flies;
What are his haunts, or which his way;
Where he would dwell, or whither stray:
Yet will I never set thee free:
For harm was meant, and harm to me.
Vain fears that vex thy virgin heart!
I'll give thee up my bow and dart;
Untangle but this cruel chain,
And freely let me fly again.
Agreed: secure my virgin heart:
Instant give up thy bow and dart:
The chain I'll in return untie;
And freely thou again shalt fly.

Thus she the captive did deliver;
The captive thus gave up his quiver.
The god disarm'd, e'er since that day
Passes his life in harmless play:
Flies round, or sits upon her breast,
A little, fluttering, idle guest.
E'er since that day the beauteous maid
Governs the world in Cupid's stead;
Directs his arrow as she wills;
Gives grief, or pleasure; spares, or kills.

CLOE HUNTING.

Behind her neck her comely tresses tied,
Her ivory quiver graceful by her side,
A-hunting Cloe went: she lost her way,
And through the woods uncertain chanc'd to stray.
Apollo passing by beheld the maid;
And, Sister, dear, bright Cynthia, turn, he said:
The hunted hind lies close in yonder brake.
Loud Cupid laugh'd, to see the god's mistake;
And laughing, cried, Learn better, great divine,
To know thy kindred, and to honour mine.
Rightly advis'd, far hence thy sister seek,
Or on Meander's bank, or Latmus' peak.
But in this nymph, my friend, my sister know:
She draws my arrows, and she bends my bow:

Fair Thames she haunts, and every neighb'ring
grove,
Sacred to soft recess, and gentle love.
Go, with thy Cynthia, hurl the pointed spear
At the rough boar, or chase the flying deer:
I and my Cloe take a nobler aim:
At human hearts we fling, nor ever miss the game.

CUPID AND GANYMEDE.

In Heaven, one holiday, you read
In wise Anacreon, Ganymede
Drew heedless Cupid in, to throw
A main, to pass an hour, or so.
The little Trojan, by the way,
By Hermes taught, play'd all the play.
The god unhappily engag'd,
By nature rash, by play enrag'd,
Complain'd, and sigh'd, and cried, and fretted;
Lost every earthly thing he betted:
In ready-money, all the store
Pick'd up long since from Danaë's shower;
A snuff-box, set with bleeding hearts,
Rubies, all pierc'd with diamond darts;
His nine-pins made of myrtle wood
(The tree in Ida's forest stood);
His bowl pure gold, the very same
Which Paris gave the Cyprian dame;

Two table-books in shagreen covers,
Fill'd with good verse from real lovers;
Merchandise rare! a billet-doux,
Its matter passionate, yet true;
Heaps of hair rings, and cipher'd seals;
Rich trifles; serious bagatelles.
What sad disorders play begets!
Desperate and mad, at length he sets
Those darts, whose points make gods adore
His might, and deprecate his power:
Those darts, whence all our joy and pain
Arise: those darts—Come, seven's the main,
Cries Ganymede: the usual trick:
Seven, slur a six; eleven, a nick.
Ill news goes fast: 'twas quickly known,
That simple Cupid was undone.
Swifter than lightning Venus flew:
Too late she found the thing too true.
Guess how the goddess greets her son:
Come hither, sirrah: no, begone;
And, hark ye, is it so indeed?
A comrade you for Ganymede?
An imp as wicked, for his age,
As any earthly lady's page;
A scandal and a scourge to Troy;
A prince's son! a blackguard boy;
A sharper, that with box and dice
Draws in young deities to vice.
All Heaven is by the ears together,
Since first that little rogue came hither:

Juno herself has had no peace:
And truly I've been favour'd less:
For Jove, as Fame reports (but Fame
Says things not fit for me to name),
Has acted ill for such a god,
And taken ways extremely odd.
And thou, unhappy child, she said,
(Her anger by her grief allay'd,)
Unhappy child, who thus hast lost
All the estate we e'er could boast;
Whither, O whither wilt thou run,
Thy name despis'd, thy weakness known?
Nor shall thy shrine on earth be crown'd;
Nor shall thy power in Heaven be own'd;
When thou, nor man, nor god canst wound.
Obedient Cupid kneeling cried,
Cease, dearest mother, cease to chide:
Gany's a cheat, and I'm a bubble.
Yet why this great excess of trouble?
The dice were false: the darts are gone:
Yet how are you or I undone?
The loss of these I can supply
With keener shafts from Cloe's eye:
Fear not, we e'er can be disgrac'd,
While that bright magazine shall last:
Your crowded altars still shall smoke;
And man your friendly aid invoke:
Jove shall again revere your power,
And rise a swan, or fall a shower.

CUPID MISTAKEN.

As after noon, one summer's day,
  Venus stood bathing in the river,
Cupid a-shooting went that way,
  New strung his bow, new fill'd his quiver.

With skill he chose his sharpest dart,
  With all his might his bow he drew;
Swift to his beauteous parent's heart
  The too well-guided arrow flew.

I faint! I die! the goddess cried;
  O cruel, couldst thou find none other,
To wreck thy spleen on? Parricide!
  Like Nero, thou hast slain thy mother.

Poor Cupid sobbing scarce could speak;
  Indeed, mamma, I did not know ye:
Alas! how easy my mistake;
  I took you for your likeness Cloe.

VENUS MISTAKEN.

When Cloe's picture was to Venus shown,
Surpris'd, the goddess took it for her own.
And what, said she, does this bold painter mean?
When was I bathing thus, and naked seen?

Pleas'd Cupid heard, and check'd his mother's pride:
And who's blind now, mamma? the urchin cried.
'Tis Cloe's eye, and cheek, and lip, and breast:
Friend Howard's genius fancied all the rest.

A SONG.

If wine and music have the power
To ease the sickness of the soul;
Let Phœbus every string explore;
And Bacchus fill the sprightly bowl.
Let them their friendly aid employ,
To make my Cloe's absence light;
And seek for pleasure, to destroy
The sorrows of this live-long night.
But she to-morrow will return;
Venus, be thou to-morrow great;
Thy myrtles strow, thy odours burn;
And meet thy fav'rite nymph in state.

Kind goddess, to no other powers
Let us to-morrow's blessings own:
Thy darling loves shall guide the hours,
And all the day be thine alone.

THE DOVE.

——Tantæne animis cœlestibus iræ?—Virg.

In Virgil's sacred verse we find,
That passion can depress or raise
The heavenly as the human mind:
Who dare deny what Virgil says?

But if they should, what our great master
Has thus laid down, my tale shall prove.
Fair Venus wept the sad disaster
Of having lost her favourite Dove.

In complaisance poor Cupid mourn'd;
His grief reliev'd his mother's pain;
He vow'd he'd leave no stone unturn'd,
But she should have her Dove again.

Though none, said he, shall yet be nam'd,
I know the felon well enough:
But be she not, mamma, condemn'd
Without a fair and legal proof.

With that, his longest dart he took,
  As constable would take his staff:
That gods desire like men to look,
  Would make e'en Heraclitus laugh.

Love's subalterns, a duteous band,
  Like watchmen round their chief appear:
Each had his lantern in his hand:
  And Venus mask'd brought up the rear.

Accoutred thus, their eager step
  To Cloe's lodging they directed:
(At once I write, alas! and weep,
  That Cloe is of theft suspected.)

Late they set out, had far to go:
  St. Dunstan's, as they pass'd, struck one.
Cloe, for reasons good, you know,
  Lives at the sober end o' th' town.

With one great peal they rap the door,
  Like footmen on a visiting day.
Folks at her house at such an hour!
  Lord! what will all the neighbours say?

The door is open: up they run:
  Nor prayers, nor threats divert their speed:
Thieves! thieves! cries Susan; we're undone;
  They'll kill my mistress in her bed.

In bed indeed the nymph had been
  Three hours: for all historians say,
She commonly went up at ten,
  Unless piquet was in the way.

She wak'd, be sure, with strange surprise,
  O Cupid, is this right or law,
Thus to disturb the brightest eyes,
  That ever slept, or ever saw?

Have you observ'd a sitting hare,
  Listening, and fearful of the storm
Of horns and hounds, clap back her ear,
  Afraid to keep, or leave her form?

Or have you mark'd a partridge quake,
  Viewing the towering falcon nigh?
She cuddles low behind the brake:
  Nor would she stay; nor dares she fly.

Then have you seen the beauteous maid;
  When gazing on her midnight foes,
She turn'd each way her frighted head,
  Then sunk it deep beneath the clothes.

Venus this while was in the chamber
  Incognito: for Susan said,
It smelt so strong of myrrh and amber—
  And Susan is no lying maid.

But since we have no present need
  Of Venus for an episode,
With Cupid let us e'en proceed;
  And thus to Cloe spoke the god:

Hold up your head: hold up your hand:
  Would it were not my lot to show ye
This cruel writ, wherein you stand
  Indicted by the name of Cloe:

For that by secret malice stirr'd,
  Or by an emulous pride invited,
You have purloin'd the fav'rite bird,
  In which my mother most delighted.

Her blushing face the lovely maid
  Rais'd just above the milk-white sheet,
A rose-tree in a lily bed
  Nor glows so red, nor breathes so sweet.

Are you not he whom virgins fear,
  And widows court? is not your name
Cupid? If so, pray come not near—
  Fair maiden, I'm the very same.

Then what have I, good Sir, to say,
  Or do with her, you call your mother?
If I should meet her in my way,
  We hardly courtesy to each other.

Diana chaste, and Hebe sweet,
Witness that what I speak is true:
I would not give my paroquet
For all the Doves that ever flew.

Yet, to compose this midnight noise,
Go freely search where'er you please:
(The rage that rais'd, adorn'd her voice)
Upon yon toilet lie my keys.

Her keys he takes; her doors unlocks:
Through wardrobe, and through closet bounces;
Peeps into every chest and box;
Turns all her furbelows and flounces.

But Dove, depend on't, finds he none;
So to the bed returns again:
And now the maiden, bolder grown,
Begins to treat him with disdain.

I marvel much, she smiling said,
Your poultry cannot yet be found:
Lies he in yonder slipper dead,
Or may be, in the tea-pot drown'd?

No, traitor, angry Love replies,
He's hid somewhere about your breast;
A place nor god nor man denies,
For Venus' Dove the proper nest.

Search then, she said, put in your hand,
  And Cynthia, dear protectress, guard me:
As guilty I, or free may stand,
  Do thou, or punish, or reward me.

But ah! what maid to Love can trust;
  He scorns, and breaks all legal power:
Into her breast his hand he thrust;
  And in a moment forc'd it lower.

O, whither do those fingers rove,
  Cries Cloe, treacherous urchin, whither?
O Venus! I shall find thy Dove,
  Says he; for sure I touch his feather.

A LOVER'S ANGER.

As Cloe came into the room t'other day,
I peevish began; where so long could you stay?
In your life-time you never regarded your hour:
You promis'd at two; and (pray look, child) 'tis four.
A lady's watch needs neither figures nor wheels:
'Tis enough, that 'tis loaded with bawbles and seals.
A temper so heedless no mortal can bear—
Thus far I went on with a resolute air.
Lord bless me, said she; let a body but speak:
Here's an ugly hard rose-bud fallen into my neck;

It has hurt me, and vex'd me to such a degree—
See here! for you never believe me; pray see,
On the left side my breast what a mark it has made!
So saying, her bosom she careless display'd:
That seat of delight I with wonder survey'd,
And forgot every word I design'd to have said.

MERCURY AND CUPID.

In sullen humour one day Jove
Sent Hermes down to Ida's grove,
Commanding Cupid to deliver
His store of darts, his total quiver;
That Hermes should the weapons break,
Or throw 'em into Lethe's lake.
Hermes, you know, must do his errand:
He found his man, produc'd his warrant;
Cupid, your darts—this very hour—
There's no contending against power.
How sullen Jupiter, just now,
I think I said; and you'll allow,
That Cupid was as bad as he:
Hear but the youngster's repartee.
Come, kinsman (said the little god),
Put off your wings, lay by your rod;
Retire with me to yonder bower,
And rest yourself for half an hour:
'Tis far indeed from hence to Heaven:

But you fly fast; and 'tis but seven.
We'll take one cooling cup of nectar;
And drink to this celestial Hector —
He break my dart, or hurt my power!
He, Leda's swan, and Danaë's shower!
Go, bid him his wife's tongue restrain,
And mind his thunder, and his rain.—
My darts! O certainly I'll give 'em:
From Cloe's eyes he shall receive 'em.
There's one, the best in all my quiver,
Twang! through his very heart and liver,
He then shall pine, and sigh, and rave:
Good lord! what bustle shall we have!
Neptune must straight be sent to sea,
And Flora summon'd twice a day:
One must find shells, and t'other flowers,
For cooling grots, and fragrant bowers,
That Cloe may be serv'd in state:
The Hours must at her toilet wait:
Whilst all the reasoning fools below
Wonder their watches go too slow,
Lybs must fly south, and Eurus east,
For jewels for her hair and breast:
No matter though their cruel haste
Sink cities, and lay forests waste.
No matter though this fleet be lost:
Or that lie wind-bound on the coast.
What, whispering in my mother's ear!
What care, that Juno should not hear!
What work among you scholar gods!

Phœbus must write him am'rous odes:
And thou, poor cousin, must compose
His letters in submissive prose;
Whilst haughty Cloe, to sustain
The honor of my mystic reign,
Shall all his gifts and vows disdain;
And laugh at your old bully's pain.
Dear couz, said Hermes in a fright,
For Heaven's sake, keep your darts! good night.

ON BEAUTY. A RIDDLE.

Resolve me, Cloe, what is this:
Or forfeit me one precious kiss.
'Tis the first offspring of the Graces;
Bears different forms in different places;
Acknowledg'd fine, where'er beheld;
Yet fancied finer, when conceal'd.
'Twas Flora's wealth, and Circe's charm;
Pandora's box of good and harm:
'Twas Mars's wish, Endymion's dream;
Apelles' draught, and Ovid's theme.
This guided Theseus through the maze;
And sent him home with life and praise.
But this undid the Phrygian boy;
And blew the flames that ruin'd Troy.
This show'd great kindness to old Greece,
And help'd rich Jason to the fleece.
This through the east just vengeance hurl'd,
And lost poor Anthony the world.

Injur'd, though Lucrece found her doom;
This banish'd tyranny from Rome.
Appeas'd though Lais gain'd her hire;
This set Persepolis on fire.
For this Alcides learn'd to spin:
His club laid down, and lion's skin.
For this Apollo deign'd to keep,
With servile care, a mortal's sheep.
For this the father of the gods,
Content to leave his high abodes,
In borrow'd figures loosely ran,
Europa's bull, and Leda's swan,
For this he reassumes the nod,
(While Semele commands the god);
Launches the bolt, and shakes the poles;
Though Momus laughs, and Juno scolds.
  Here listening Cloe smil'd and said;
Your riddle is not hard to read:
I guess it—fair one, if you do;
Need I, alas! the theme pursue?
For this thou see'st, for this I leave,
Whate'er the world thinks wise or grave,
Ambition, business, friendship, news,
My useful books, and serious Muse.
For this I willingly decline
The mirth of feasts, and joys of wine;
And choose to sit and talk with thee,
(As thy great orders may decree)
Of cocks and bulls, and flutes and fiddles,
Of idle tales, and foolish riddles.

THE QUESTION. TO LISETTA.

WHAT nymph should I admire, or trust,
But Cloe, beauteous Cloe, just?
What nymph should I desire to see,
But her who leaves the plain for me?
To whom should I compose the lay,
But her who listens when I play?
To whom, in song, repeat my cares,
But her who in my sorrow shares?
For whom should I the garland make,
But her who joys the gift to take,
And boasts she wears it for my sake?
In love am I not fully blest?
Lisetta, pr'ythee tell the rest.

LISETTA'S REPLY.

SURE, Cloe just, and Cloe fair,
Deserves to be your only care:
But when you and she to-day
Far into the wood did stray,
And I happen'd to pass by,
Which way did you cast your eye?
But when your cares to her you sing,
Yet dare not tell her whence they spring;

Does it not more afflict your heart,
That in those cares she bears a part?
When you the flowers for Cloe twine,
Why do you to her garland join
The meanest bud that falls from mine?
Simplest of swains! the world may see,
Whom Cloe loves, and who loves me.

THE GARLAND.

The pride of every grove I chose,
The violet sweet, and lily fair,
The dappled pink, and blushing rose,
To deck my charming Cloe's hair.

At morn the nymph vouchsaf'd to place
Upon her brow the various wreath;
The flowers less blooming than her face,
The scent less fragrant than her breath.

The flowers she wore along the day:
And every nymph and shepherd said,
That in her hair they look'd more gay
Than glowing in their native bed.

Undrest at evening when she found
Their odours lost, their colours past;
She chang'd her look, and on the ground
Her garland and her eye she cast.

That eye dropt sense distinct and clear,
  As any Muse's tongue could speak,
When from its lid a pearly tear
  Ran trickling down her beauteous cheek.

Dissembling what I knew too well,
  My love, my life, said I, explain
This change of humour: pr'ythee, tell:
  That falling tear—What does it mean?

She sigh'd; she smil'd: and to the flowers
  Pointing, the lovely moralist said:
See, friend, in some few fleeting hours,
  See yonder, what a change is made.

Ah me! the blooming pride of May,
  And that of beauty are but one:
At morn both flourish bright and gay,
  Both fade at evening, pale, and gone.

At dawn poor Stella danc'd and sung;
  The amorous youth around her bow'd;
At night her fatal knell was rung;
  I saw, and kiss'd her in her shroud.

Such as she is, who died to-day,
  Such I, alas! may be to-morrow;
Go, Damon, bid thy Muse display
  The justice of thy Cloe's sorrow.

THE LADY WHO OFFERS HER LOOKING-GLASS TO VENUS.[1]

Venus, take my votive glass;
Since I am not what I was,
What from this day I shall be,
Venus, let me never see.

CLOE JEALOUS.

Forbear to ask me, why I weep;
  Vex'd Cloe to her shepherd said;
'Tis for my two poor straggling sheep
  Perhaps, or for my squirrel dead.

For mind I what you late have writ?
  Your subtle questions, and replies;
Emblems, to teach a female wit
  The ways, where changing Cupid flies.

Your riddle purpos'd to rehearse
  The general power that beauty has;
But why did no peculiar verse
  Describe one charm of Cloe's face?

[1] Taken from an epigram of Plato. See Rambler, Number 143.

The glass, which was at Venus' shrine,
  With such mysterious sorrow laid:
The garland (and you call it mine)
  Which show'd how youth and beauty fade.

Ten thousand trifles light as these
  Nor can my rage, nor anger move:
She should be humble, who would please;
  And she must suffer, who can love.

When in my glass I chanc'd to look;
  Of Venus what did I implore?
That every grace which thence I took,
  Should know to charm my Damon more.

Reading thy verse; Who heeds, said I,
  If here or there his glances flew?
O free for ever be his eye,
  Whose heart to me is always true.

My bloom indeed, my little flower
  Of beauty quickly lost its pride;
For, sever'd from its native bower,
  It on thy glowing bosom died.

Yet car'd I not what might presage,
  Or withering wreath, or fleeting youth;
Love I esteem'd more strong than age,
  And time less permanent than truth.

Why then I weep, forbear to know:
  Fall uncontroll'd my tears, and free:
O Damon! 'tis the only woe
  I ever yet conceal'd from thee.

The secret wound with which I bleed
  Shall lie wrapt up, e'en in my hearse;
But on my tombstone thou shalt read
  My answer to thy dubious verse.

ANSWER TO CLOE JEALOUS,

IN THE SAME STYLE. THE AUTHOR SICK.

Yes, fairest proof of Beauty's power,
  Dear idol of my panting heart,
Nature points this my fatal hour:
  And I have liv'd; and we must part.

While now I take my last adieu,
  Heave thou no sigh, nor shed a tear;
Lest yet my half-clos'd eye may view
  On earth an object worth its care.

From Jealousy's tormenting strife
  For ever be thy bosom freed:
That nothing may disturb thy life,
  Content I hasten to the dead.

Yet when some better-fated youth
Shall with his amorous parley move thee;
Reflect one moment on his truth
Who, dying thus, persists to love thee.

A BETTER ANSWER.

Dear Cloe, how blubber'd is that pretty face;
Thy cheek all on fire, and thy hair all uncurl'd:
Pr'y thee quit this caprice; and (as old Falstaff says)
Let us e'en talk a little like folks of this world.

How canst thou presume, thou hast leave to destroy
The beauties, which Venus but lent to thy keeping?
Those looks were design'd to inspire love and joy:
More ord'nary eyes may serve people for weeping.

To be vex'd at a trifle or two that I writ,
Your judgment at once, and my passion you wrong:
You take that for fact, which will scarce be found wit:
Odds life! must one swear to the truth of a song?

What I speak, my fair Cloe, and what I write, shows
The difference there is betwixt nature and art:
I court others in verse; but I love thee in prose:
And they have my whimsies, but thou hast my heart.

The god of us verse-men (you know child) the sun,
  How after his journeys he sets up his rest:
If at morning o'er earth 'tis his fancy to run;
  At night he declines on his Thetis's breast.

So when I am wearied with wandering all day,
  To thee, my delight, in the evening I come:
No matter what beauties I saw in my way;[1]
  They were but my visits, but thou art my home.

Then finish, dear Cloe, this pastoral war;
  And let us, like Horace and Lydia, agree:
For thou art a girl as much brighter than her,
  As he was a poet sublimer than me.

PALLAS AND VENUS. AN EPIGRAM.

The Trojan swain had judg'd the great dispute,
And beauty's power obtain'd the golden fruit;
When Venus, loose in all her naked charms,
Met Jove's great daughter clad in shining arms.
The wanton goddess view'd the warlike maid
From head to foot, and tauntingly she said:

[1] My heart with her but, as guest-wise, sojourn'd;
And now to Helen it is home return'd,
There to remain.——
Midsummer Night's Dream, A. iii. S. 2.

Yield, sister; rival, yield: naked, you see,
I vanquish: guess how potent I should be,
If to the field I came in armour drest; [crest!
Dreadful, like thine, my shield, and terrible my
The warrior goddess with disdain replied:
Thy folly, child, is equal to thy pride:
Let a brave enemy for once advise,
And Venus (if 'tis possible) be wise.
Thou to be strong must put off every dress;
Thy only armour is thy nakedness:
And more than once, (or thou art much belied)
By Mars himself that armour has been tried.

TO A YOUNG GENTLEMAN IN LOVE.

A TALE.

From public noise and factious strife,
From all the busy ills of life,
Take me, my Celia, to thy breast,
And lull my wearied soul to rest.
For ever, in this humble cell,
Let thee and I, my fair one, dwell;
None enter else, but Love——and he
Shall bar the door, and keep the key.
To painted roofs, and shining spires
(Uneasy seats of high desires)
Let the unthinking many crowd,
That dare be covetous and proud:

In golden bondage let them wait,
And barter happiness for state.
But oh! my Celia, when thy swain
Desires to see a court again,
May Heaven around this destin'd head
The choicest of its curses shed!
To sum up all the rage of Fate,
In the two things I dread and hate;
Mayst thou be false, and I be great!
Thus, on his Celia's panting breast,
Fond Celadon his soul express'd;
While with delight the lovely maid
Receiv'd the vows, she thus repaid:
  Hope of my age, joy of my youth,
Blest miracle of love and truth!
All that could e'er be counted mine,
My love and life, long since are thine:
A real joy I never knew,
Till I believ'd thy passion true:
A real grief I ne'er can find,
Till thou prov'st perjur'd or unkind.
Contempt, and poverty, and care,
All we abhor, and all we fear,
Blest with thy presence, I can bear.
Through waters, and through flames I'll go,
Sufferer and solace of thy woe:
Trace me some yet unheard-of way,
That I thy ardour may repay;
And make my constant passion known,
By more than woman yet has done.

Had I a wish that did not bear
The stamp and image of my dear;
I'd pierce my heart through every vein,
And die to let it out again.
No; Venus shall my witness be,
(If Venus ever lov'd like me)
That for one hour I would not quit
My shepherd's arms, and this retreat,
To be the Persian monarch's bride,
Partner of all his power and pride;
Or rule in regal state above,
Mother of gods, and wife of Jove.
O happy these of human race!
But soon, alas! our pleasures pass.
He thank'd her on his bended knee;
Then drank a quart of milk and tea:
And leaving her ador'd embrace,
Hasten'd to court to beg a place.
While she, his absence to bemoan,
The very moment he was gone,
Call'd Thyrsis from beneath the bed!
Where all this time he had been hid.

MORAL.

While men have these ambitious fancies;
And wanton wenches read romances;
Our sex will—What? out with it. Lie;
And theirs in equal strains reply.

The moral of the tale I sing
(A posy for a wedding ring)
In this short verse will be confin'd:
Love is a jest, and vows are wind.

AN ENGLISH PADLOCK.

Miss Danaë, when fair and young,
(As Horace has divinely sung)
Could not be kept from Jove's embrace
By doors of steel, and walls of brass.
The reason of the thing is clear;
Would Jove the naked truth aver:
Cupid was with him of the party,
And show'd himself sincere and hearty:
For, give that whipster but his errand,
He takes my Lord Chief Justice' warrant;
Dauntless as death away he walks;
Breaks the doors open; snaps the locks;
Searches the parlour, chamber, study;
Nor stops till he has culprit's body.
  Since this has been authentic truth,
By age deliver'd down to youth;
Tell us, mistaken husband, tell us,
Why so mysterious, why so jealous?
Does the restraint, the bolt, the bar
Make us less curious, her less fair?
The spy, which does this treasure keep,

Does she ne'er say her prayers, nor sleep?
Does she to no excess incline?
Does she fly music, mirth, and wine?
Or have not gold and flattery power
To purchase one unguarded hour?
  Your care does farther yet extend:
That spy is guarded by your friend.—
But has this friend nor eye, nor heart?
May he not feel the cruel dart,
Which, soon or late, all mortals feel?
May he not, with too tender zeal,
Give the fair pris'ner cause to see,
How much he wishes she were free?
May he not craftily infer
The rules of friendship too severe,
Which chain him to a hated trust;
Which make him wretched, to be just?
And may not she, this darling she,
  Youthful and healthy, flesh and blood,
Easy with him, ill us'd by thee,
  Allow this logic to be good?
  Sir, will your questions never end?
I trust to neither spy nor friend.
In short, I keep her from the sight
Of every human face.—She'll write.
From pen and paper she's debarr'd.—
Has she a bodkin and a card?
She'll prick her mind.—She will you say:
But how shall she that mind convey?
I keep her in one room: I lock it:

The key (look here) is in this pocket.
The key-hole, is that left? most certain,
She'll thrust her letter through—Sir Martin.
  Dear angry friend, what must be done?
Is there no way?—There is but one.
Send her abroad; and let her see,
That all this mingled mass, which she,
Being forbidden, longs to know,
Is a dull farce, an empty show,
Powder, and pocket-glass, and beau;
A staple of romance and lies,
False tears, and real perjuries:
Where sighs and looks are bought and sold;
And love is made but to be told;
Where the fat bawd, and lavish heir
The spoils of ruin'd beauty share:
And youth, seduc'd from friends and fame,
Must give up age to want and shame.
Let her behold the frantic scene,
The women wretched, false the men:
And when, these certain ills to shun,
She would to thy embraces run;
Receive her with extended arms:
Seem more delighted with her charms:
Wait on her to the park and play:
Put on good humour; make her gay:
Be to her virtues very kind;
Be to her faults a little blind;
Let all her ways be unconfin'd;
And clap your padlock—on her mind.

HANS CARVEL.

HANS CARVEL, impotent and old,
Married a lass of London mould:
Handsome? enough; extremely gay:
Lov'd music, company, and play:
High flights she had, and wit at will;
And so her tongue lay seldom still:
For in all visits who but she,
To argue, or to repartee?
  She made it plain, that human passion
Was order'd by predestination;
That if weak women went astray,
Their stars were more in fault than they:
Whole tragedies she had by heart;
Enter'd into Roxana's part:
To triumph in her rival's blood,
The action certainly was good.
How like a vine young Ammon curl'd!
Oh that dear conqueror of the world!
She pitied Betterton in age,
That ridicul'd the god-like rage.
  She, first of all the town, was told,
Where newest India things were sold:
So in a morning, without bodice,
Slip sometimes out to Mrs. Thody's;
To cheapen tea, to buy a screen:
What else could so much virtue mean?

For to prevent the least reproach,
Betty went with her in the coach.
  But when no very great affair
Excited her peculiar care,
She without fail was wak'd at ten;
Drank chocolate, then slept again:
At twelve she rose; with much ado
Her clothes were huddled on by two;
Then, does my lady dine at home?
Yes, sure;—but is the Colonel come?
Next, how to spend the afternoon,
And not come home again too soon;
The Change, the City, or the Play,
As each was proper for the day:
A turn in summer to Hyde Park,
When it grew tolerably dark.
  Wife's pleasure causes husband's pain:
Strange fancies come in Hans's brain:
He thought of what he did not name;
And would reform, but durst not blame.
At first he therefore preach'd his wife
The comforts of a pious life:
Told her how transient beauty was;
That all must die, and flesh was grass:
He bought her sermons, psalms, and graces;
And doubled down the useful places.
But still the weight of worldly care
Allow'd her little time for prayer:
And Cleopatra[1] was read o'er,

[1] Cleopatra is a novel, much read by the ladies in the last century.

While Scot,[1] and Wake,[2] and twenty more,
That teach one to deny oneself,
Stood unmolested on the shelf.
An untouch'd Bible grac'd her toilet:
No fear that thumb of hers should spoil it.
In short, the trade was still the same:
The dame went out, the colonel came.
  What's to be done? Poor Carvel cried:
Another battery must be tried:
What if to spells I had recourse?
'Tis but to hinder something worse.
The end must justify the means:
He only sins who ill intends:
Since therefore 'tis to combat evil,
'Tis lawful to employ the devil.
  Forthwith the devil did appear
(For name him, and he's always near),
Not in the shape in which he plies
At miss's elbow when she lies;
Or stands before the nursery doors,
To take the naughty boy that roars:
But, without saucer-eye or claw,
Like a grave barrister at law.
  Hans Carvel, lay aside your grief,
The devil says; I bring relief.
Relief, says Hans: pray let me crave

1 Dr. John Scot, rector of St. Giles in the Fields, and author of the Christian Life, in 5 vols.

2 Dr. William Wake, afterwards archbishop of Canterbury.

Your name, Sir,—Satan—Sir, your slave;
I did not look upon your feet:
You'll pardon me:——Ay, now I see't:
And pray, Sir, when came you from hell?
Our friends there, did you leave them well?
All well; but pr'ythee, honest Hans,
(Says Satan) leave your complaisance:
The truth is this: I cannot stay
Flaring in sunshine all the day:
For, *entre nous*, we hellish sprites
Love more the fresco of the nights;
And oftener our receipts convey
In dreams, than any other way.
I tell you therefore as a friend,
Ere morning dawns, your fears shall end:
Go then this evening, master Carvel,
Lay down your fowls, and broach your barrel;
Let friends and wine dissolve your care;
Whilst I the great receipt prepare:—
To-night I'll bring it, by my faith;
Believe for once what Satan saith.
  Away went Hans: glad? not a little;
Obey'd the devil to a tittle;
Invited friends some half a dozen,
The colonel and my lady's cousin.
The meat was serv'd; the bowls were crown'd;
Catches were sung; and healths went round;
Barbadoes waters for the close;
Till Hans had fairly got his dose:
The colonel toasted to the best:

The Dame mov'd off, to be undrest:
The chimes went twelve: the guests withdrew:
But when, or how, Hans hardly knew.
Some modern anecdotes aver,
He nodded in his elbow chair;
From thence was carried off to bed:
John held his heels, and Nan his head.
My lady was disturb'd: new sorrow!
Which Hans must answer for to-morrow.
  In bed then view this happy pair;
And think how Hymen triumph'd there.
Hans fast asleep as soon as laid,
The duty of the night unpaid:
The waking dame, with thoughts opprest,
That made her hate both him and rest;
By such a husband, such a wife!
'Twas Acme's and Septimius' life:
The lady sigh'd: the lover snor'd:
The punctual devil kept his word:
Appear'd to honest Hans again;
But not at all by madam seen:
And giving him a magic ring,
Fit for the finger of a king;
Dear Hans, said he, this jewel take,
And wear it long for Satan's sake:
'Twill do your business to a hair:
For, long as you this ring shall wear,
As sure as I look over Lincoln,
That ne'er shall happen which you think on.
  Hans took the ring with joy extreme;

(All this was only in a dream)
And, thrusting it beyond his joint,
'Tis done, he cried: Iv'e gain'd my point.—
What point, said she, you ugly beast?
You neither give me joy nor rest:
'Tis done.—What's done, you drunken bear?
You've thrust your finger G-d knows where.

A DUTCH PROVERB.

Fire, water, woman, are man's ruin:
Says wise professor Vander Brüin.
By flames a house I hir'd was lost
Last year, and I must pay the cost.
This spring the rains o'erflow'd my ground:
And my best Flanders mare was drown'd.
A slave I am to Clara's eyes:
The gipsy knows her power, and flies.
Fire, water, woman, are my ruin:
And great thy wisdom, Vander Brüin.

PAULO PURGANTI AND HIS WIFE:

AN HONEST, BUT A SIMPLE PAIR.

Est enim quiddam, idque intelligitur in omni virtute, quod deceat: quod cogitatione magis à virtute potest quàm re separari. Cic. de Off. L. 2.

BEYOND the fix'd and settled rules
Of vice and virtue in the schools,
Beyond the letter of the law,
Which keeps our men and maids in awe,
The better sort should set before 'em
A grace, a manner, a decorum;
Something, that gives their acts a light;
Makes 'em not only just, but bright;
And sets them in that open fame,
Which witty malice cannot blame.
For 'tis in life, as 'tis in painting:
Much may be right, yet much be wanting;
From lines drawn true, our eye may trace
A foot, a knee, a hand, a face:
May justly own the picture wrought
Exact to rule, exempt from fault:
Yet, if the colouring be not there,
The Titian stroke, the Guido air;
To nicest judgment show the piece;
At best 'twill only not displease:

It would not gain on Jersey's eye :
Bradford would frown, and set it by.
  Thus in the picture of our mind
The action may be well design'd;
Guided by law, and bound by duty ;
Yet want this *Je ne sçay quoi* of beauty :
And though its error may be such,
  As [1]Knags and Burgess cannot hit;
It yet may feel the nicer touch
  Of Wycherley's or Congreve's wit.
  What is this talk? replies a friend,
And where will this dry moral end?
The truth of what you here lay down
By some example should be shown.—
With all my heart,—for once ; read on.
An honest, but a simple pair
(And twenty other I forbear)
May serve to make this thesis clear.
  A doctor of great skill and fame,
Paulo Purganti was his name,
Had a good, comely, virtuous wife;
No woman led a better life :
She to intrigues was e'en hard-hearted:
She chuckled when a bawd was carted;
And thought the nation ne'er would thrive,
Till all the whores were burnt alive.
  On married men, that dar'd be bad,
She thought no mercy should be had;

[1] Two divines. Knags was Lecturer of St. Giles in the Field; Burgess, a Dissenter.

They should be hang'd, or starv'd or flead,
Or serv'd like Romish priests in Swede.
In short, all lewdness she defied:
And stiff was her parochial pride.
  Yet, in an honest way, the dame
Was a great lover of that same;
And could from scripture take her cue,
That husbands should give wives their due.
  Her prudence did so justly steer
Between the gay and the severe,
That if in some regards she chose
To curb poor Paulo in too close;
In others she relax'd again,
And govern'd with a looser rein.
  Thus though she stricty did confine
The doctor from excess of wine;
With oysters, eggs, and vermicelli,
She, let him almost burst his belly:
Thus drying coffee was denied;
But chocolate that loss supplied:
And for tobacco (who could bear it),
Filthy concomitant of claret!
(Blest revolution!) one might see
Eringo roots, and bohea tea.
  She often set the doctor's band,
And strok'd his beard, and squeez'd his hand:
Kindly complain'd, that after noon
He went to pore on books too soon:
She held it wholesomer by much,
To rest a little on the couch:—

About his waist in bed a-nights
She clung so close—for fear of sprites.
  The Doctor understood the call;
But had not always wherewithal.
  The lion's skin too short, you know
(As Plutarch's Morals finely show),
Was lengthen'd by the fox's tail;
And art supplies, where strength may fail.
  Unwilling then, in arms to meet
The enemy he could not beat;
He strove to lengthen the campaign,
And save his forces by chicane.
Fabius, the Roman chief, who thus
By fair retreat grew Maximus,
Shows us, that all the warrior can do
With force inferior, is CUNCTANDO.
  One day then, as the foe drew near,
With love, and joy, and life, and dear;
Our don, who knew this tittletattle
Did, sure as trumpet, call to battle:
Thought it extremely *à propos*,
To ward against the coming blow:
To ward: but how? Ay, there's the question;
Fierce the assault, unarm'd the bastion.
  The doctor feign'd a strange surprise:
He felt her pulse; he view'd her eyes;
That beat too fast, these roll'd too quick;
She was, he said, or would be sick;
He judg'd it absolutely good,
That she should purge and cleanse her blood.

Spa waters for that end were got:
If they pass'd easily or not,
What matters it? the lady's fever
Continued violent as ever.
  For a distemper of this kind,
(Blackmore[1] and Hans[2] are of my mind,)
If once it youthful blood infects,
And chiefly of the female sex,
Is scarce remov'd by pill or potion;
Whate'er might be our doctor's notion.
  One luckless night then, as in bed
The doctor and the dame were laid;
Again this cruel fever came,
High pulse, short breath, and blood in flame.
What measures shall poor Paulo keep
  With madam in this piteous taking?
She, like Macbeth, has murder'd sleep,
  And won't allow him rest though waking.
Sad state of matters! when we dare
Nor ask for peace, nor offer war;
Nor Livy nor Comines have shown,
What in this juncture may be done.
Grotius might own, that Paulo's case is
Harder than any which he places
Amongst his Belli and his Pacis.
  He strove, alas! but strove in vain,
By dint of logic to maintain,
That all the sex was born to grieve,
Down to her ladyship from Eve.

[1] Sir Richard Blackmore. [2] Sir Edward Hannes.

He rang'd his tropes, and preach'd up patience;
Back'd his opinion with quotations,
Divines and moralists; and run ye on
Quite through from Seneca to Bunyan.[1]
As much in vain he bid her try
To fold her arms, and close her eye;
Telling her, rest would do her good,
If any thing in nature could:
So held the Greeks quite down from Galen,
Masters and princes of their calling:
So all our modern friends maintain
(Though no great Greeks) in Warwick-lane.
  Reduce, my Muse, the wandering song:
A tale should never be too long.
  The more he talk'd, the more she burn'd,
And sigh'd, and toss'd, and groan'd, and turn'd:
At last, I wish, said she, my dear—
(And whisper'd something in his ear.)
You wish! wish on, the doctor cries:
Lord! when will womankind be wise?
What, in your waters? are you mad?
Why poison is not half so bad.
I'll do it—but I give you warning:
You'll die before to-morrow morning.—
'Tis kind, my dear, what you advise;
The lady with a sigh replies!
But life, you know, at best is pain;
And death is what we should disdain.

[1] John Bunyan, author of the Pilgrim's Progress.

So do it, therefore, and adieu:
For I will die for love of you.—
Let wanton wives by death be scar'd:
But, to my comfort, I'm prepar'd.

THE LADLE.

The sceptics think, 'twas long ago,
Since gods came down *incognito:*
To see who were their friends or foes,
And how our actions fell or rose:
That since they gave things their beginning,
And set this whirligig a spinning;
Supine they in their Heaven remain,
Exempt from passion, and from pain.
And frankly leave us human elves,
To cut and shuffle for ourselves:
To stand or walk, to rise or tumble,
As matter, and as motion jumble.
The poets now, and painters hold
This thesis both absurd and bold:
And your good-natur'd gods, they say,
Descend some twice or thrice a-day:
Else all these things we toil so hard in,
Would not avail one single farthing:
For, when the hero we rehearse,
To grace his actions and our verse;

'Tis not by dint of human thought,
That to his Latium he is brought;
Iris descends by Fate's commands,
To guide his steps through foreign lands:
And Amphitrite clears the way
From rocks and quicksands in the sea.
And if you see him in a sketch
(Though drawn by Paulo or Carache),
He shews not half his force and strength,
Strutting in armour, and at length:
That he may take his proper figure,
The piece must yet be four yards bigger:
The nymphs conduct him to the field;
One holds his sword, and one his shield:
Mars, standing by, asserts his quarrel;
And Fame flies after with a laurel.
These points, I say, of speculation
(As 'twere to save or sink the nation)
Men idly-learned will dispute,
Assert, object, confirm, refute:
Each mighty angry, mighty right,
With equal arms sustains the fight;
Till now no umpire can agree 'em:
So both draw off and sing *Te Deum.*
Is it in *equilibrio*,
If deities descend or no?
Then let the affirmative prevail,
As requisite to form my tale:
For by all parties 'tis confest,
That those opinions are the best,

Which in their nature most conduce
To present ends, and private use.
Two gods came therefore from above,
One Mercury, the other Jove:
The humour was (it seems) to know,
If all the favours they bestow,
Could from our own perverseness ease us;
And if our wish enjoy'd would please us.
Discoursing largely on this theme,
O'er hills and dales their godships came;
Till, wellnigh tir'd and almost night,
They thought it proper to alight.
Note here, that it as true as odd is,
That in disguise a god or goddess
Exerts no supernatural powers;
But acts on maxims much like ours.
They spied at last a country farm,
Where all was snug, and clean, and warm;
For woods before and hills behind
Secur'd it both from rain and wind:
Large oxen in the fields were lowing:
Good grain was sow'd; good fruit was growing:
Of last year's corn in barns great store;
Fat turkeys gobbling at the door:
And wealth (in short) with peace consented
That people here should live contented:
But did they in effect do so?
Have patience, friend, and thou shalt know.
The honest farmer and his wife,
To years declin'd from prime of life,

Had struggled with the marriage noose,
As almost every couple does:
Sometimes, my plague! sometimes, my darling!
Kissing to-day, to-morrow snarling;
Jointly submitting to endure
That evil, which admits no cure.
Our gods the outward gates unbarr'd:
Our farmer met 'em in the yard;
Thought they were folks that lost their way,
And ask'd them civilly to stay:
Told 'em, for supper, or for bed
They might go on, and be worse sped.
So said, so done: the gods consent:
All three into the parlour went:
They compliment; they sit; they chat;
Fight o'er the wars; reform the state:
A thousand knotty points they clear,
Till supper and my wife appear.
Jove made his leg, and kiss'd the dame:
Obsequious Hermes did the same.
Jove kiss'd the farmer's wife, you say
He did—but in an honest way:
Oh! not with half that warmth and life,
With which he kiss'd Amphitryon's wife.
Well then, things handsomely were serv'd:
My mistress for the strangers carv'd.
How strong the beer, how good the meat,
How loud they laugh'd, how much they eat,
In epic sumptuous would appear;
Yet shall be pass'd in silence here:

For I should grieve to have it said,
That, by a fine description led,
I made my episode too long,
Or tir'd my friend, to grace my song.
The grace-cup serv'd, the cloth away,
Jove thought it time to show his play:
Landlord and landlady, he cried,
Folly and jesting laid aside,
That ye thus hospitably live,
And strangers with good cheer receive,
Is mighty grateful to your betters,
And makes e'en gods themselves your debtors.
To give this thesis plainer proof,
You have to-night beneath your roof
A pair of gods (nay, never wonder):
This youth can fly, and I can thunder.
I'm Jupiter, and he Mercurius,
My page, my son indeed, but spurious.
Form then three wishes, you and madam;
And sure, as you already had 'em,
The things desir'd in half an hour
Shall all be here, and in your power.
Thank ye, great gods, the woman says:
Oh! may your altars ever blaze!
A ladle for our silver dish
Is what I want, is what I wish,—
A ladle! cries the man, a ladle!
Odzooks, Corisca, you have pray'd ill;
What should be great, you turn to farce;
I wish the ladle in your a—.

With equal grief and shame my muse
The sequel of the tale pursues;
The ladle fell into the room,
And stuck in old Corisca's bum.
Our couple weep two wishes past,
And kindly join to form the last;
To ease the woman's awkward pain,
And get the ladle out again.

MORAL.

This commoner has worth and parts,
Is prais'd for arms, or lov'd for arts:
His head aches for a coronet:
And who is bless'd that is not great?
Some sense, and more estate, kind Heaven
To this well-lotted peer has given:
What then? he must have rule and sway;
And all is wrong, 'till he's in play.
The miser must make up his plum,
And dares not touch the hoarded sum;
The sickly dotard wants a wife,
To draw off his last dregs of life.
Against our peace we arm our will:
Amidst our plenty, something still
For horses, houses, pictures, planting,
To thee, to me, to him is wanting.
That cruel something unpossessed
Corrodes and leavens all the rest.

That something, if we could obtain,
Would soon create a future pain;
And to the coffin, from the cradle,
'Tis all a Wish, and all a Ladle.

WRITTEN AT PARIS. MDCC.

IN THE BEGINNING OF ROBE'S GEOGRAPHY.

Of all that William rules, or Robe
Describes, great Rhea, of thy globe;
When or on post-horse, or in chaise,
With much expense, and little ease,
My destin'd miles I shall have gone,
By Thames or Maese, by Po or Rhone,
And found no foot of earth my own;
Great Mother, let me once be able
To have a garden, house, and stable;
That I may read, and ride, and plant,
Superior to desire, or want;
And as health fails, and years increase,
Sit down, and think, and die in peace.
Oblige thy favourite undertakers
To throw me in but twenty acres:
This number sure they may allow;
For pasture ten, and ten for plow:
'Tis all that I would wish, or hope,
For me and John, and Nell, and Crop.

Then, as thou wilt, dispose the rest
(And let not Fortune spoil the jest)
To those, who at the market-rate
Can barter honour for estate.
  Now if thou grant'st me my request,
To make thy votary truly blest,
Let curst revenge, and saucy pride
To some bleak rock far off be tied;
Nor e'er approach my rural seat,
To tempt me to be base and great.
  And, Goddess, this kind office done,
Charge Venus to command her son,
(Wherever else she lets him rove)
To shun my house, my field, my grove:
Peace cannot dwell with hate or love.
  Hear, gracious Rhea, what I say:
And thy petitioner shall pray.

WRITTEN IN THE BEGINNING OF MEZERAY'S HISTORY OF FRANCE.

WHATE'ER thy countrymen have done
By law and wit, by sword and gun,
  In thee is faithfully recited:
And all the living world, that view
Thy work, give thee the praises due,
  At once instructed and delighted.

Yet for the fame of all these deeds,
What beggar in the Invalides,
  With lameness broke, with blindness smitten,
Wish'd ever decently to die,
To have been either Mezeray,
  Or any monarch he has written?

It's strange, dear author, yet it true is,
That, down from Pharamond to Louis,
  All covet life, yet call it pain:
All feel the ill, yet shun the cure:
Can sense this paradox endure?
  Resolve me, Cambray, or Fontaine.

The man in graver tragic known
(Though his best part long since was done)
  Still on the stage desires to tarry:
And he who play'd the Harlequin,
After the jest still loads the scene
  Unwilling to retire, though weary.

WRITTEN IN THE NOUVEAUX INTERETS

DES PRINCES DE L'EUROPE.

BLEST be the princes, who have fought
  For pompous names, or wide dominion:
Since by their error we are taught,
  That happiness is but opinion.

ADRIANI MORIENTIS AD ANIMAM SUAM.

Animula, vagula, blandula,
Hospes, comesque corporis,
Quæ nunc abibis in loca,
Pallidula, rigida, nudula ?
Nec, ut soles, dabis joca.

BY MONSIEUR FONTENELLE.

Ma petite âme, ma mignonne,
Tu t'en vas donc, ma fille, et Dieu sçache où tu vas :
Tu pars seulette, nuë, et tremblotante, helas !
Que deviendra ton humeur folichonne !
Que deviendront tant de jolis ébats !

IMITATED.

Poor little pretty, fluttering thing,
  Must we no longer live together ?
And dost thou prune thy trembling wing ;
  To take thy flight thou know'st not whither ?
Thy humourous vein, thy pleasing folly
  Lies all neglected, all forgot :
And pensive, wavering, melancholy,
  Thou dread'st and hop'st thou know'st not what.

A PASSAGE IN THE MORIÆ ENCOMIUM OF ERASMUS IMITATED.

In awful pomp, and melancholy state,
See settled Reason on the judgment seat;
Around her crowd Distrust, and Doubt, and Fear,
And thoughtful Foresight, and tormenting Care:
Far from the throne, the trembling Pleasures stand,
Chain'd up, or exil'd by her stern command.
Wretched her subjects, gloomy sits the queen;
Till happy Chance reverts the cruel scene:
And apish Folly with her wild resort
Of wit and jest disturbs the solemn court.
See the fantastic minstrelsy advance,
To breathe the song, and animate the dance.
Blest the usurper! happy the surprise!
Her mimic postures catch our eager eyes:
Her jingling bells affect our captive ear;
And in the sights we see, and sounds we hear,
Against our judgment she our sense employs;
The laws of troubled Reason she destroys,
And in their place rejoices to indite
Wild schemes of mirth, and plans of loose delight.

TO DR. SHERLOCK,[1]

ON HIS PRACTICAL DISCOURSE CONCERNING DEATH.

Forgive the Muse, who, in unhallow'd strains,
The Saint one moment from his God detains:
For sure, whate'er you do, where'er you are,
'Tis all but one good work, one constant prayer:
Forgive her; and entreat that God, to whom
Thy favour'd vows with kind acceptance come,
To raise her notes to that sublime degree,
Which suits a song of piety and thee.
  Wondrous good man! whose labours may repel
The force of sin, may stop the rage of hell:
Thou, like the Baptist, from thy God was sent,
The crying voice, to bid the world repent.
  The Youth shall study, and no more engage
Their flattering wishes for uncertain age;
No more with fruitless care, and cheated strife,
Chase fleeting Pleasure through this maze of life:
Finding the wretched all they here can have,
But present food, and but a future grave:
Each, great as Philip's victor son, shall view
This abject world, and, weeping, ask a new.
Decrepid Age shall read thee, and confess
Thy labours can assuage, where medicines cease;

[1] Dr. William Sherlock, master of the Temple; father of Dr. Thomas Sherlock, late Bishop of London.

Shall bless thy words, their wounded soul's relief,
The drops that sweeten their last dregs of life;
Shall look to Heaven, and laugh at all beneath;
Own riches gather'd, trouble; fame, a breath;
And life an ill, whose only cure is death.
  Thy even thoughts with so much plainness flow,
Their sense untutor'd infancy may know:
Yet to such height is all that plainness wrought,
Wit may admire, and letter'd Pride be taught:
Easy in words, thy style in sense sublime,
  On its blest steps each age and sex may rise;
'Tis like the ladder in the Patriarch's dream,
  Its foot on earth, its height above the skies,
Diffus'd its virtue, boundless is its power;
'Tis public health, and universal cure;
Of heavenly manna 'tis a second feast;
A nation's food, and all to every taste.
  To its last height mad Britain's guilt was rear'd;
And various death for various crimes she fear'd.
With your kind work her drooping hopes revive;
You bid her read, repent, adore, and live:
You wrest the bolt from Heaven's avenging hand;
Stop ready death, and save a sinking land.
  O! save us still: still bless us with thy stay:
O! want thy Heaven, till we have learnt the way:
Refuse to leave thy destin'd charge too soon:
And for the church's good, defer thy own.
O! live: and let thy works urge our belief;
Live to explain thy doctrine by thy life;
Till future infancy, baptiz'd by thee,

Grow ripe in years, and old in piety;
Till Christians, yet unborn, be taught to die.
  Then in full age, and hoary holiness,
Retire, great teacher! to thy promis'd bliss:
Untouch'd thy tomb, uninjur'd be thy dust,
As thy own fame among the future just;
Till in last sounds the dreadful trumpet speaks;
Till Judgment calls; and quicken'd Nature wakes:
Till through the utmost earth, and deepest sea,
Our scatter'd atoms find their destin'd way,
In haste to clothe their kindred souls again,
Perfect our state, and build immortal man:
Then fearless thou, who well sustain'st the fight,
To paths of Joy, or tracts of endless light,
Lead up all those who heard thee, and believ'd;
'Midst thy own flock, great shepherd, be receiv'd;
And glad all Heaven with millions thou hast sav'd.

CARMEN SECULARE, FOR THE YEAR MDCC.

TO THE KING.

Adspice, venturo lætantur ut omnia sæclo:
O mihi tam longæ maneat pars ultima vitæ,
Spiritus et, quantum sat erit tua dicere facta!
VIRG. Eclog. 4.

THY elder look, great Janus, cast
Into the long records of ages past:
Review the years in fairest action dress'd
With noted white, superior to the rest;

Æras deriv'd, and chronicles begun,
From empires founded, and from battles won;
Show all the spoils by valiant kings achiev'd;
And groaning nations by their arms reliev'd;
The wounds of patriots in their country's cause,
And happy power sustain'd by wholesome laws;
In comely rank call every merit forth;
Imprint on every act its standard worth;
The glorious parallels then downward bring
To modern wonders, and to Britain's king:
With equal justice and historic care,
Their laws, their toils, their arms with his compare:
Confess the various attributes of fame
Collected and complete in William's name:
  To all the listening world relate,
    (As thou dost his story read),
  That nothing went before so great,
    And nothing greater can succeed.

Thy native Latium was thy darling care,
Prudent in peace, and terrible in war:
The boldest virtues that have govern'd earth
From Latium's fruitful womb derive their birth.
  Then turn to her fair written page;
From dawning childhood to establish'd age,
  The glories of her empire trace;
Confront the heroes of thy Roman race;
And let the justest palm the victor's temples grace.

The son of Mars reduc'd the trembling swains,

And spread his empire o'er the distant plains:
But yet the Sabines' violated charms
Obscur'd the glory of his rising arms.
Numa the rights of strict religion knew;
On every altar laid the incense due;
Unskill'd to dart the pointed spear,
Or lead the forward youth to noble war.
Stern Brutus was with too much horror good,
Holding his fasces stain'd with filial blood.
Fabius was wise, but with excess of care
He sav'd his country; but prolong'd the war.
While Decius, Paulus, Curius, greatly fought,
And by their strict examples taught,
How wild desires should be controll'd,
And how much brighter virtue was, than gold:
They scarce their swelling thirst of fame could hide;
And boasted poverty with too much pride.
Excess in youth made Scipio less rever'd;
And Cato dying, seem'd to own, he fear'd.
Julius with honour tam'd Rome's foreign foes;
But patriots fell, ere the dictator rose.
And, while with clemency Augustus reign'd,
The monarch was ador'd; the city chain'd.

With justest honour be their merits dress'd;
But be their failings too confess'd:
Their virtue, like their Tyber's flood,
Rolling its course, design'd the country's good.
But oft the torrent's too impetuous speed
From the low earth tore some polluting weed;

And with the blood of Jove there always ran,
Some viler part, some tincture of the man.

Few virtues after these so far prevail,
But that their vices more than turn the scale:
Valour grown wild by pride, and power by rage,
Did the true charms of majesty impair;
Rome by degrees advancing more in age,
Shew'd sad remains of what had once been fair;
Till Heaven a better race of men supplies:
And glory shoots new beams from western skies.

Turn then to Pharamond, and Charlemain,
And the long heroes of the Gallic strain;
Experienc'd chiefs, for hardy prowess known,
And bloody wreaths in venturous battles won.
From the first William, our great Norman king,
The bold Plantagenets, and Tudors bring;
Illustrious virtues, who by turns have rose
In foreign fields to check Britannia's foes;
With happy laws her empire to sustain,
And with full power assert her ambient main.
But sometimes too industrious to be great,
Nor patient to expect the turns of fate,
They open'd camps deform'd by civil fight,
And made proud conquest trample over right;
Disparted Britain mourn'd their doubtful sway,
And dreaded both when neither would obey.

From Didier and imperial Adolph trace

The glorious offspring of the Nassau race,
Devoted lives to public liberty;
The chief still dying, or the country free.
Then see the kindred blood of Orange flow,
From warlike Cornet, through the loins of Beau;
Through Chalon next, and there with Nassau join,
From Rhone's fair banks transplanted to the Rhine.
Bring next the royal list of Stuarts forth,
Undaunted minds that rul'd the rugged north;
Till Heaven's decrees by ripening times are shown;
Till Scotland's kings ascend the English throne;
And the fair rivals live for ever one.

Janus, mighty deity,
Be kind: and, as thy searching eye
Does our modern story trace,
Finding some of Stuart's race
Unhappy, pass their annals by:
No harsh reflection let remembrance raise:
Forbear to mention what thou canst not praise:
But as thou dwell'st upon that heavenly name,[1]
To grief for ever sacred, as to fame,
Oh! read it to thyself; in silence weep;
And thy convulsive sorrows inward keep;
Lest Britain's grief should waken at the sound;
And blood gush fresh from her eternal wound.

Whither wouldst thou further look?

[1] Mary.

Read William's acts, and close the ample book:
Peruse the wonders of his dawning life:
  How, like Alcides, he began;
With infant patience calm'd seditious strife,
And quell'd the snakes which round his cradle ran.

  Describe his youth, attentive to alarms,
By dangers form'd, and perfected in arms:
When conq'ring, mild; when conquer'd, not disgrac'd;
By wrongs not lessen'd, nor by triumphs rais'd:
  Superior to the blind events
  Of little human accidents;
And constant to his first decree,
To curb the proud, to set the injur'd free;
To bow the haughty neck, and raise the suppliant knee.

His opening years to riper manhood bring;
And see the hero perfect in the king:
Imperious arms by manly reason sway'd,
And power supreme by free consent obey'd;
With how much haste his mercy meets his foes:
And how unbounded his forgiveness flows;
With what desire he makes his subjects bless'd,
His favours granted ere his throne address'd:
What trophies o'er our captiv'd hearts he rears,
By arts of peace more potent, than by wars:
How o'er himself, as o'er the world, he reigns,
His morals strengthening what his law ordains.

Through all his thread of life already spun,
Becoming grace and proper action run:
The piece by Virtue's equal hand is wrought,
Mixt with no crime, and shaded with no fault;
No footsteps of the victor's rage
Left in the camp where William did engage:
No tincture of the monarch's pride
Upon the royal purple spied:
His fame, like gold, the more 'tis tried,
The more shall its intrinsic worth proclaim;
Shall pass the combat of the searching flame,
And triumph o'er the vanquish'd heat,
For ever coming out the same,
And losing not its lustre nor its weight.

Janus, be to William just:
To faithful history his actions trust:
Command her, with peculiar care
To trace each toil, and comment every war:
His saving wonders bid her write
In characters distinctly bright;
That each revolving age may read
The Patriot's piety, the Hero's deed;
And still the sire inculcate to his son
Transmissive lessons of the king's renown;
That William's glory still may live;
When all that present art can give,
The pillar'd marble, and the tablet brass,
Mouldering, drop the victor's praise:
When the great monuments of his power

Shall now be visible no more ; [flood ;
When Sambre shall have chang'd her winding
And children ask, where Namur stood.

Namur, proud city, how her towers were arm'd !
How she contemn'd the approaching foe :
Till she by William's trumpets was alarm'd,
And shook, and sunk, and fell beneath his blow.
Jove and Pallas, mighty powers,
Guided the hero to the hostile towers.
Perseus seem'd less swift in war,
When, wing'd with speed, he flew through air.
Embattled nations strive in vain
The hero's glory to restrain :
Streams arm'd with rocks, and mountains red with fire
In vain against his force conspire.
Behold him from the dreadful height appear !
And lo ! Britannia's lions waving there.

Europe freed, and France repell'd,
The hero from the height beheld :
He spake the word, that war and rage should cease :
He bid the Maese and Rhine in safety flow ;
And dictated a lasting peace
To the rejoicing world below.
To rescu'd states, and vindicated crowns,
His equal hand prescrib'd their ancient bounds ;
Ordain'd, whom every province should obey ;
How far each monarch should extend his sway ;

Taught 'em how clemency made power rever'd;
And that the prince belov'd was truly fear'd.
Firm by his side unspotted Honour stood,
Pleas'd to confess him not so great as good;
His head with brighter beams fair Virtue deck'd,
Than those which all his numerous crowns reflect:
Establish'd Freedom clapp'd her joyful wings;
Proclaim'd the first of men, and best of kings.

Whither would the Muse aspire
With Pindar's rage, without his fire?
Pardon me, Janus, 'twas a fault,
Created by too great a thought:
Mindless of the god and day,
I from thy altars, Janus, stray,
From thee, and from myself, borne far away.
The fiery Pegasus disdains
To mind the rider's voice, or hear the reins:
When glorious fields and opening camps he views;
He runs with an unbounded loose:
Hardly the Muse can sit the headstrong horse;
Nor would she, if she could, check his impetuous force;
With the glad noise the cliffs and valleys ring;
While she through earth and air pursues the king.

She now beholds him on the Belgic shore;
Whilst Britain's tears his ready help implore,
Dissembling for her sake his rising cares,
And with wise silence pondering vengeful wars.

She through the raging ocean now
Views him advancing his auspicious prow;
Combating adverse winds and winter seas,
Sighing the moments that defer our ease;
Daring to wield the sceptre's dangerous weight,
And taking the command, to save the state;
Though ere the doubtful gift can be secur'd,
New wars must be sustain'd, new wounds endur'd.

Through rough Ierne's camps she sounds alarms,
And kingdoms yet to be redeem'd by arms;
In the dank marshes finds her glorious theme,
And plunges after him thro' Boyne's fierce stream.
She bids the Nereids run with trembling haste,
To tell old Ocean how the Hero past.
The god rebukes their fear, and owns the praise
Worthy that arm, whose empire he obeys.

Back to his Albion she delights to bring
The humblest victor, and the kindest king.
Albion with open triumph would receive
Her hero, nor obtains his leave:
Firm he rejects the altars she would raise;
And thanks the zeal, while he declines the praise.
Again she follows him through Belgia's land,
And countries often sav'd by William's hand;
Hears joyful nations bless those happy toils,
Which freed the people, but return'd the spoils.
In various views she tries her constant theme;
Finds him in councils, and in arms the same;

When certain to o'ercome, inclin'd to save,
Tardy to vengeance, and with mercy brave.

Sudden another scene employs her sight;
She sets her hero in another light:
Paints his great mind superior to success,
Declining conquest, to establish peace;
She brings Astrea down to earth again,
And quiet, brooding o'er his future reign.

Then with unweary wing the goddess soars
East, over Danube and Propontis' shores;
Where jarring empires, ready to engage,
Retard their armies, and suspend their rage;
Till William's word, like that of Fate, declares,
If they shall study peace, or lengthen wars.
How sacred his renown for equal laws,
To whom the world defers its common cause!
How fair his friendships, and his leagues how just,
Whom every nation courts, whom all religions trust!

From the Mæotis to the Northern sea,
The goddess wings her desperate way;
See the young Muscovite,[1] the mighty head,
Whose sovereign terror forty nations dread,
Enamour'd with a greater monarch's praise,
And passing half the earth to his embrace:
She in his rule beholds his Volga's force,
O'er precipices with impetuous sway

1 Peter the Great.

Breaking, and as he rolls his rapid course,
Drowning, or bearing down, whatever meets his
way.
But her own king she likens to his Thames,
With gentle course devolving fruitful streams:
Serene yet strong, majestic yet sedate,
Swift without violence, without terror great.
Each ardent nymph the rising current craves;
Each shepherd's prayer retards the parting waves:
The vales along the bank their sweets disclose:
Fresh flowers for ever rise: and fruitful harvest
grows.

Yet whither would th' adventurous goddess go?
Sees she not clouds, and earth, and main below?
Minds she the dangers of the Lycian coast,
And fields, where mad Bellerophon was lost?
Or is her towering flight reclaim'd,
By seas from Icarus's downfall nam'd?
Vain is the call, and useless the advice:
To wise persuasion deaf, and human cries,
Yet upwards she incessant flies;
Resolv'd to reach the high empyrean sphere,
And tell great Jove, she sings his image here;
To ask for William an olympic crown,
To Chromius' strength and Theron's speed un-
known:
Till, lost in trackless fields of shining day,
Unable to discern the way,
Which Nassau's virtue only could explore,

Untouch'd, unknown, to any Muse before;
She, from the noble precipices thrown,
Comes rushing with uncommon ruin down.
  Glorious attempt! unhappy fate!
The song too daring, and the theme too great!
  Yet rather thus she wills to die,
Than in continued annals live, to sing
A second hero, or a vulgar king;
  And with ignoble safety fly
In sight of earth, along a middle sky.

To Janus' altars, and the numerous throng,
  That round his mystic temple press,
  For William's life, and Albion's peace,
Ambitious Muse reduce the roving song.
  Janus, cast thy forward eye
Future, into great Rhea's pregnant womb;
  Where young ideas brooding lie,
And tender images of things to come:
Till by thy high commands releas'd,
Till by thy hand in proper atoms dress'd,
In decent order they advance to light;
Yet then too swiftly fleet by human sight;
And meditate too soon their everlasting flight.

Nor beaks of ships in naval triumph borne,
Nor standards from the hostile ramparts torn,
  Nor trophies brought from battles won,
Nor oaken wreath, nor mural crown,
  Can any future honours give

To the victorious monarch's name:
The plenitude of William's fame
Can no accumulated stores receive.
Shut then, auspicious god, thy sacred gate,
And make us happy, as our king is great.
Be kind, and with a milder hand,
Closing the volume of the finish'd age,
(Though noble, 'twas an iron page)
A more delightful leaf expand,
Free from alarms, and fierce Bellona's rage:
Bid the great months begin their joyful round,
By Flora some, and some by Ceres crown'd;
Teach the glad hours to scatter as they fly,
Soft quiet, gentle love, and endless joy:
Lead forth the years for peace and plenty fam'd,
From Saturn's rule, and better metal nam'd,

Secure by William's care let Britain stand;
Nor dread the bold invader's hand:
From adverse shores in safety let her hear
Foreign calamity, and distant war;
Of which let her, great Heaven, no portion bear!
Betwixt the nations let her hold the scale,
And as she wills, let either part prevail:
Let her glad valleys smile with wavy corn:
Let fleecy flocks her rising hills adorn:
Around her coast let strong defence be spread:
Let fair abundance on her breast be shed:
And heavenly sweets bloom round the goddess' head.

Where the white towers and ancient roofs did stand.
Remains of [1]Wolsey's, or great Henry's hand,
To age now yielding, or devour'd by flame,
Let a young phœnix raise her towering head;
Her wings with lengthen'd honour let her spread,
And by her greatness shew her builder's fame:
August and open, as the hero's mind,
Be her capacious courts design'd:
Let every sacred pillar bear
Trophies of arms, and monuments of war.
The king shall there in Parian marble breathe,
His shoulder bleeding fresh: and at his feet
Disarm'd shall lie the threatening Death:
(For so was saving Jove's decree complete.)
Behind, that angel shall be plac'd, whose shield
Sav'd Europe in the blow repell'd:
On the firm basis, from his oozy bed,
Boyne shall raise his laurell'd head;
And his immortal stream be known,
Artfully waving through the wounded stone.

And thou, imperial Windsor, stand enlarg'd,
With all the monarch's trophies charg'd:
Thou, the fair Heaven, that dost the stars inclose,

[1] Whitehall, once belonging to the Archbishop of York. It was taken from Cardinal Wolsey by Henry the 8th, who made great improvements therein, and converted it into a royal palace. In 1698 the whole of it, except the Banqueting House, was destroyed by fire, and hath not since been rebuilt.

Which William's bosom wears, or hand bestows
On the great champions who support his throne,
And virtues nearest to his own.

Round Ormond's knee, thou tiest the mystic string,
That makes the knight companion to the king.
From glorious camps return'd, and foreign fields,
Bowing before thy sainted warrior's shrine,
Fast by his great forefather's coats, and shields
Blazon'd from Bohun's, or from Butler's line,
He hangs his arms; nor fears those arms should shine
With an unequal ray; or that his deed
With paler glory should recede,
Eclips'd by theirs, or lessen'd by the fame
E'en of his own maternal Nassau's name.

Thou smiling see'st great Dorset's worth confest,
The ray distinguishing the patriot's breast:
Born to protect and love, to help and please;
Sovereign of wit, and ornament of peace.
O! long as breath informs this fleeting frame,
Ne'er let me pass in silence Dorset's name;
Ne'er cease to mention the continued debt
Which the great patron only would forget,
And duty, long as life, must study to acquit.

Renown'd in thy records shall Ca'ndish stand,
Asserting legal power, and just command:
To the great house thy favour shall be shown,
The father's star transmissive to the son.

From thee the Talbot's and the Seymour's race
Inform'd, their sire's immortal steps shall trace:
  Happy, may their sons receive
The bright reward, which thou alone canst give.

And if a god these lucky numbers guide;
If sure Apollo o'er the verse preside;
Jersey, belov'd by all (for all must feel
  The influence of a form and mind,
Where comely grace and constant virtue dwell,
Like mingled streams, more forcible when join'd)—
  Jersey shall at thy altars stand;
  Shall there receive the azure band,
  That fairest mark of favour and of fame,
  Familiar to the Villiers' name.

Science to raise, and knowledge to enlarge,
  Be our great master's future charge;
To write his own memoirs, and leave his heirs
High schemes of government, and plans of wars;
By fair rewards our noble youth to raise
To emulous merit, and to thirst of praise;
To lead them out from ease ere opening dawn,
Through the thick forest and the distant lawn,
Where the fleet stag employs their ardent care,
And chases give them images of war.
To teach them vigilance by false alarms;
Inure them in feign'd camps to real arms;
Practise them now to curb the turning steed,
Mocking the foe; now to his rapid speed

To give the rein, and in the full career,
To draw the certain sword, or send the pointed spear.

Let him unite his subjects' hearts,
Planting societies for peaceful arts;
Some that in nature shall true knowledge found;
And by experiment make precept sound;
Some that to morals shall recall the age,
And purge from vicious dross the sinking stage;
Some that with care true eloquence shall teach,
And to just idioms fix our doubtful speech:
That from our writers distant realms may know,
The thanks we to our monarch owe;
And schools profess our tongue through every land,
That has invok'd his aid, or blest his hand.

Let his high power the drooping Muses rear,
The Muses only can reward his care:
'Tis they that guard the great Atrides' spoils;
'Tis they that still renew Ulysses' toils:
To them by smiling Jove 'twas given, to save
Distinguish'd patriots from the common grave;
To them, great William's glory to recall,
When statues moulder, and when arches fall.
Nor let the Muses, with ungrateful pride,
The sources of their treasure hide:
The Hero's virtue does the string inspire,
When with big joy they strike the living lyre:
On William's fame their fate depends:
With him the song begins: with him it ends.

From this bright effluence of his deed
They borrow that reflected light,
With which the lasting lamp they feed,
Whose beams dispel the damps of envious night.

Through various climes, and to each distant pole,
In happy tides let active commerce roll:
Let Britain's ships export an annual fleece,
Richer than Argos brought to ancient Greece:
Returning loaden with the shining stores,
Which lie profuse on either India's shores.
As our high vessels pass their watery way,
Let all the naval world due homage pay;
With hasty reverence their top-honours lower,
Confessing the asserted power,
To whom by fate 'twas given, with happy sway
To calm the earth, and vindicate the sea.

Our prayers are heard, our masters' fleets shall go
As far as winds can bear, or waters flow,
New lands to make, new Indies to explore,
In worlds unknown to plant Britannia's power;
Nations yet wild by precept to reclaim,
And teach them arms, and arts, in William's name.

With humble joy, and with respectful fear
The listening people shall his story hear,
The wounds he bore, the dangers he sustain'd,
How far he conquer'd, and how well he reign'd;
Shall own his mercy equal to his fame,

And form their children's accents to his name,
Inquiring how, and when from Heaven he came.
Their regal tyrants shall with blushes hide
Their little lusts of arbitrary pride,
  Nor bear to see their vassals tied;
When William's virtues raise their opening thought,
His forty years for public freedom fought,
  Europe by his hand sustain'd,
  His conquest by his piety restrain'd,
And o'er himself the last great triumph gain'd.

No longer shall their wretched zeal adore
  Ideas of destructive power,
Spirits that hurt, and godheads that devour:
New incense they shall bring, new altars raise,
And fill their temples with a stranger's praise;
When the great father's character they find
Visibly stamp'd upon the hero's mind;
And own a present Deity confest,
In valour that preserv'd, and power that blest.

Through the large convex of the azure sky
(For thither nature casts our common eye)
Fierce meteors shoot their arbitrary light:
And comets march with lawless horror bright:
These hear no rule, no righteous order own;
Their influence dreaded as their ways unknown:
Through threaten'd lands they wild destruction
    throw,
Till ardent prayer averts the public woe:

But the bright orb that blesses all above,
The sacred fire, the real son of Jove,
Rules not his actions by capricious will;
Nor by ungovern'd power declines to ill:
Fix'd by just laws he goes for ever right:
Man knows his course, and thence adores his light.

O Janus! would entreated Fate conspire
To grant what Britain's wishes could require;
Above, that sun should cease his way to go,
Ere William cease to rule, and bless below:
But a relentless destiny
Urges all that e'er was born:
Snatch'd from her arms, Britannia once must mourn
The demi-god: the earthly half must die.
Yet if our incense can your wrath remove;
If human prayers avail on minds above;
Exert, great God, thy interest in the sky;
Gain each kind Power, each guardian Deity;
That conquer'd by the public vow,
They bear the dismal mischief far away:
O! long as utmost nature may allow,
Let them retard the threaten'd day!
Still be our master's life thy happy care:
Still let his blessings with his years increase:
To his laborious youth consum'd in war,
Add lasting age, adorn'd and crown'd with peace:
Let twisted olive bind those laurels fast,
Whose verdue must for ever last!

Long let this growing era bless his sway:
And let our sons his present rule obey:
On his sure virtue long let earth rely:
And late let the imperial eagle fly,
To bear the hero through his father's sky,
To Leda's twins, or he whose glorious speed,
On foot prevail'd, or he who tam'd the steed;
To Hercules, at length absolv'd by Fate
From earthly toil, and above envy great:
To Virgil's theme, bright Cytherea's son,
Sire of the Latian, and the British throne:
  To all the radiant names above,
  Rever'd by men, and dear to Jove.
  Late, Janus, let the Nassau-star,
New-born, in rising majesty appear,
    To triumph over vanquish'd night,
  And guide the prosperous mariner
With everlasting beams of friendly light.

AN ODE.

INSCRIBED TO THE MEMORY OF THE HONOURABLE COLONEL GEORGE VILLIERS,[1]

DROWNED IN THE RIVER PIAVA, IN THE COUNTRY OF FRIULI, MDCCIII. IN IMITATION OF HORACE, ODE 28, LIB. I.

Te maris et terræ numeroque carentis arenæ
Mensorem cohibent, Archyta, &c.

Say, dearest Villiers, poor departed friend,
(Since fleeting life thus suddenly must end)
Say, what did all thy busy hopes avail,
That anxious thou from pole to pole didst sail;
Ere on thy chin the springing beard began
To spread a doubtful down, and promise man?
What profited thy thoughts, and toils, and cares,
In vigour more confirm'd, and riper years?
To wake ere morning dawn to loud alarms,
And march till close of night in heavy arms;
To scorn the summer's suns and winter's snows,
And search through every clime thy country's foes!

1 Colonel George Villiers was in the marine service. When this accident happened to him he was accompanied by William Courtenay, Esq., son of Sir William Courtenay, a captain in his regiment, and both shared the same fate. They had been out on an excursion to see the country.

That thou mightst Fortune to thy side engage;
That gentle Peace might quell Bellona's rage;
And Anna's bounty crown her soldier's hoary age?
  In vain we think that free-will'd man has power
To hasten or protract th' appointed hour.
Our term of life depends not on our deed:
Before our birth our funeral was decreed.
Nor aw'd by foresight, nor misled by chance,
Imperious Death directs his ebon lance;
Peoples great Henry's tombs, and leads up
        Holbein's dance.
  Alike must every state, and every age
Sustain the universal tyrant's rage:
For neither William's power, nor Mary's charms,
Could, or repel, or pacify his arms:
Young Churchill[1] fell, as life began to bloom:
And Bradford's[2] trembling age expects the tomb.
Wisdom and eloquence in vain would plead
One moment's respite for the learned head:
Judges of writings and of men have died;
Mæcenas, Sackville, Socrates, and Hyde:
And in their various turns their sons must tread
Those gloomy journeys which their sires have led.

[1] John Churchill, Marquis of Blandford, only son of John, Duke of Marlborough by Sarah his duchess. He died 10th March, 1702, aged 16, and was buried at King's College chapel, Cambridge.

[2] Francis Newport, Earl of Bradford. He died 19th September, 1708.

The ancient sage, who did so long maintain
That bodies die, but souls return again,
With all the births and deaths he had in store,
Went out Pythagoras, and came no more.
And modern Asgyll,[1] whose capricious thought
Is yet with stores of wilder notions fraught,
Too soon convinc'd, shall yield that fleeting breath,
Which play'd so idly with the darts of death.
Some from the stranded vessel force their way;
Fearful of Fate, they meet it in the sea:
Some who escape the fury of the wave,
Sicken on earth, and sink into a grave:
In journeys or at home, in war or peace,
By hardships many, many fall by ease.
Each changing season does its poison bring,
Rheums chill the winter, agues blast the spring:

1 John Asgyll, Esq., a lawyer of some eminence, but more remarkable for the very extraordinary publication here alluded to. He was a member of the English parliament for Bramber in Sussex. In the year 1700 he published a treatise, entitled, "An argument proving that according to the covenant of eternal life revealed in the scriptures, man may be translated hence into that eternal life without passing through death, although the human nature of Christ himself could not be thus translated till he had passed through death." Being involved in many perplexing lawsuits, and much reduced in his circumstances, the House of Commons made this pamphlet a pretence for expelling him in September, 1707. His affairs afterwards continued to grow worse, and he passed the remainder of his life in the rules of the King's Bench, or Fleet. He died within the former on the 10th of November, 1738, when he was considerably above fourscore years of age.

Wet, dry, cold, hot, at the appointed hour,
All act subservient to the tyrant's power:
And when obedient nature knows his will,
A fly, a grapestone, or a hair can kill.
For restless Proserpine for ever treads
In paths unseen, o'er our devoted heads;
And on the spacious land, and liquid main,
Spreads slow disease, or darts afflictive pain:
Variety of deaths confirm her endless reign.
On curst Piava's banks the goddess stood,
Shew'd her dire warrant to the rising flood;
When what I long must love, and long must mourn,
With fatal speed was urging his return;
In his dear country to disperse his care,
And arm himself by rest for future war;
To chide his anxious friends' officious fears,
And promise to their joys his elder years.
Oh! destin'd head; and oh! severe decree;
Nor native country thou, nor friend shall see:
Nor war hast thou to wage, nor year to come:
Impending death is thine, and instant doom.
Hark! the imperious goddess is obey'd:
Winds murmur, snows descend, and waters spread;
Oh! kinsman, friend—Oh! vain are all the cries
Of human voice; strong destiny replies:
Weep you on earth: for he shall sleep below:
Thence none return; and thither all must go.
Whoe'er thou art, whom choice or business leads
To this sad river, or the neigbouring meads;
If thou mayst happen on the dreary shores,

To find the object which this verse deplores ;
Cleanse the pale corpse with a religious hand
From the polluting weed and common sand;
Lay the dead hero graceful in a grave ;
(The only honour he can now receive)
And fragrant mould upon his body throw :
And plant the warrior laurel o'er his brow:
Light lie the earth; and flourish green the bough.
So may just Heaven secure thy future life
From foreign dangers, and domestic strife !
And when the infernal judge's dismal power
From the dark urn shall throw thy destin'd hour ;
When yielding to the sentence, breathless thou
And pale shalt lie, as what thou buriest now;
May some kind friend the piteous object see,
And, equal rites perform to that which once was
thee.

PROLOGUE.

SPOKEN AT COURT BEFORE THE QUEEN, ON HER MAJESTY'S BIRTH DAY, MDCCIV.

SHINE forth, ye planets, with distinguish'd light,
As when ye hallow'd first this happy night:
Again transmit your friendly beams to earth :
As when Britannia joy'd for Anna's birth :
And thou, propitious star, whose sacred power
Presided o'er the monarch's natal hour,

Thy radiant voyages for ever run,
Yielding to none but Cynthia and the Sun:
With thy fair aspect still illustrate Heaven:
Kindly preserve what thou hast greatly given:
Thy influence for thy Anna we implore;
Prolong one life; and Britain asks no more:
For virtue can no ampler power express,
Than to be great in war, and good in peace:
For thought no higher wish of bliss can frame,
Than to enjoy that virtue still the same.
Entire and sure the monarch's rule must prove,
Who founds her greatness on her subjects' love;
Who does our homage for our good require;
And orders that which we should first desire:
Our vanquish'd wills that pleasing force obey,
Her goodness takes our liberty away,
And haughty Britain yields to arbitrary sway.
  Let the young Austrian then her terrors bear,
Great as he is, her delegate in war:
Let him in thunder speak to both his Spains,
That in these dreadful isles a woman reigns.
While the bright queen does on her subjects shower
The gentle blessings of her softer power;
Give sacred morals to a vicious age,
To temples zeal, and manners to the stage;
Bids the chaste Muse without a blush appear;
And wit be that which Heaven and she may hear.
  Minerva thus to Perseus lent her shield;
Secure of conquest, sent him to the field:
The hero acted what the queen ordain'd:

So was his fame complete, and Andromede un-
chain'd.
Meantime amidst her native temples sate
The goddess, studious of her Grecian's fate,
Taught them in laws and letters to excel,
In acting justly, and in writing well.
Thus whilst she did her various power dispose,
The world was freed from tyrants, wars, and woes :
Virtue was taught in verse, and Athen's glory rose.

A LETTER
TO MONSIEUR BOILEAU DESPREAUX, OCCASIONED BY THE VICTORY AT BLENHEIM, MDCCIV.

——Cupidum, pater optime, vires
Deficiunt: neque enim quivis horrentia pilis
Agmina, nec fractâ pereuntes cuspide Gallos.
HOR. Sat. I. L. 2.

SINCE hir'd for life, thy servile Muse must sing
Successive conquests, and a glorious king;
Must of a man immortal vainly boast,
And bring him laurels, whatsoe'er they cost:
What turn wilt thou employ, what colours lay
On the event of that superior day,
In which one English subject's prosperous hand
(So Jove did will; so Anna did command)
Broke the proud column of thy master's praise,
Which sixty winters had conspir'd to raise?

From the lost field a hundred standards brought
Must be the work of Chance, and Fortune's fault:
Bavaria's stars must be accus'd, which shone
That fatal day the mighty work was done,
With rays oblique upon the Gallic sun.
Some demon envying France misled the fight;
And Mars mistook, though Louis order'd right.
When thy[1] young Muse invok'd the tuneful Nine,
To say how Louis did not pass the Rhine,
What work had we with Wageninghen, Arnheim,
Places that could not be reduc'd to rhyme!
And though the poet made his last efforts,
Wurts—who could mention in heroic—Wurts?
But, tell me, hast thou reason to complain
Of the rough triumphs of the last campaign;
The Danube rescued, and the empire sav'd,
Say, is the majesty of verse retriev'd?
And would it prejudice thy softer vein,
To sing the princes, Louis and Eugene?
Is it too hard in happy verse to place
The Vans and Vanders of the Rhine and Maes?
Her warriors Anna sends from Tweed and Thames,
That France may fall by more harmonious names,
Canst thou not Hamilton or Lumley bear?
Would Ingoldsby or Palmes offend thy ear?
And is there not a sound in Marlborough's name,
Which thou, and all thy brethren ought to claim,
Sacred to verse, and sure of endless fame?

1 Epistre 4. du Sr. Boileau Despreaux au Roy.
En vain, pour te loüer, &c.

Cutts is in metre something harsh to read:
Place me the valiant Gouram in his stead:
Let the intention make the number good:
Let generous Sylvius speak for honest Wood.
And though rough Churchill scarce in verse will
stand,
So as to have one rhyme at his command:
With ease the bard reciting Blenheim's plain,
May close the verse, remembering but the Dane.
I grant, old friend, old foe, (for such we are
Alternate as the chance of peace and war)
That we poetic folks, who must restrain
Our measur'd sayings in an equal chain,
Have troubles utterly unknown to those
Who let their fancy loose in rambling prose.
For instance now, how hard is it for me
To make my matter and my verse agree!
"In one great day on Hochstet's fatal plain,
French and Bavarians twenty thousand slain;
Push'd through the Danube to the shores of
Styx
Squadrons eighteen, battalions twenty-six:
Officers captive made and private men,
Of these twelve hundred, of those thousands ten.
Tents, ammunition, colours, carriages,
Cannon, and kettle-drums!"—sweet numbers these.
But is it thus you English bards compose?
With Runic lays thus tag insipid prose?
And when you should your heroes' deeds rehearse,
Give us a commissary's list in verse?

Why, faith! Despreaux, there's sense in what you say:
I told you where my difficulty lay:
So vast, so numerous were great Blenheim's spoils,
They scorn the bounds of verse, and mock the Muse's toils.
To make the rough recital aptly chime,
Or bring the sum of Gallia's loss to rhyme,
'Tis mighty hard: what poet would essay
To count the streamers of my Lord Mayor's-day?
To number all the several dishes drest
By honest Lamb, last coronation feast?
Or make arithmetic and epic meet,
And Newton's thoughts in Dryden's style repeat?
O Poet, had it been Apollo's will,
That I had shar'd a portion of thy skill:
Had this poor breast receiv'd the heavenly beam;
Or could I hope my verse might reach my theme;
Yet, Boileau, yet the labouring Muse should strive,
Beneath the shades of Marlborough's wreaths to live:
Should call aspiring gods to bless her choice;
And to their favourite strains exalt her voice,
Arms and a queen to sing; who, great and good,
From peaceful Thames to Danube's wandering flood,
Sent forth the terror of her high commands,
To save the nations from invading hands,
To prop fair Liberty's declining cause,
And fix the jarring world with equal laws.

The queen should sit in Windsor's sacred grove,
Attended by the gods of war and love:
Both should with equal zeal her smiles implore,
To fix her joys, or to extend her power.
Sudden, the Nymphs and Tritons should appear;
And as great Anna's smiles dispel their fear,
With active dance should her observance claim;
With vocal shell should sound her happy name.
Their master Thames should leave the neighb'ring shore,
By his strong anchor known, and silver oar;
Should lay his ensigns at his sovereign's feet,
And audience mild with humble grace entreat.
To her, his dear defence, he should complain,
That whilst he blesses her indulgent reign;
Whilst furthest seas are by his fleets survey'd,
And on his happy banks each India laid;
His brethren Maese, and Waal, and Rhine, and Saar,
Feel the hard burden of oppressive war:
That Danube scarce retains his rightful course
Against two rebel armies' neighbouring force:
And all must weep sad captives to the Seine,
Unless unchain'd and freed by Britain's queen.
The valiant sovereign calls her general forth;
Neither recites her bounty, nor his worth:
She tells him, he must Europe's fate redeem,
And by that labour merit her esteem:
She bids him wait her to the sacred hall;
Shows him prince Edward, and the conquer'd Gaul;
Fixing the bloody cross upon his breast,
Says, he must die, or succour the distress'd:

Placing the saint an emblem by his side,
She tells him Virtue arm'd must conquer lawless
Pride.
The hero bows obedient, and retires:
The queen's commands exalt the warrior's fires.
His steps are to the silent woods inclin'd,
The great design revolving in his mind:
When to his sight a heavenly form appears:
Her hand a palm, her head a laurel wears.
Me, she begins, the fairest child of Jove,
Below for ever sought, and bless'd above;
Me, the bright source of wealth, and power, and
fame;
(Nor need I say, Victoria is my name)
Me the great father down to thee has sent:
He bids me wait at thy distinguish'd tent,
To execute what Anna's wish would have:
Her subject thou, I only am her slave.
Dare then, thou much belov'd by smiling fate,
For Anna's sake, and in her name, be great:
Go forth, and be to distant nations known,
My future favourite, and my darling son.
At Schellenbergh I'll manifest sustain
Thy glorious cause; and spread my wings again,
Conspicuous o'er thy helm, in Blenheim's plain.
The goddess said, nor would admit reply;
But cut the liquid air, and gain'd the sky.
His high commission is through Britain known:
And thronging armies to his standard run,
He marches thoughtful, and he speedy sails:
(Bless him, ye seas! and prosper him, ye gales!)

Belgia receives him welcome to her shores,
And William's death with lessen'd grief deplores:
His presence only must retrieve that loss;
Marlborough to her must be what William was.
So when great Atlas, from these low abodes
Recall'd, was gather'd to his kindred gods;
Alcides respited by prudent fate,
Sustain'd the ball, nor droop'd beneath the weight.
Secret and swift behold the chief advance;
Sees half the empire join'd, and friend to France:
The British general dooms the fight; his sword
Dreadful he draws: the captains wait the word.
Anne and St. George! the charging hero cries:
Shrill echo from the neighbouring wood replies,
Anne and St. George.—At that auspicious sign
The standards move; the adverse armies join.
Of eight great hours, Time measures out the sands;
And Europe's fate in doubtful balance stands;
The ninth, Victoria comes:—o'er Marlborough's head
Confess'd she sits; the hostile troops recede:
Triumphs the goddess, from her promise freed.
The eagle, by the British lion's might
Unchain'd and free, directs her upward flight:
Nor did she e'er with stronger pinions soar
From Tyber's banks, than now from Danube's shore.
Fir'd with the thoughts which these ideas raise,
And great ambition of my country's praise;
The English Muse should like the Mantuan rise,

Scornful of earth and clouds, should reach the skies,
With wonder (though with envy still) pursued by
human eyes.
But we must change the style—just now I said,
I ne'er was master of the tuneful trade;
Or the small genius which my youth could boast,
In prose and business lies extinct and lost.
Bless'd if I may some younger muse excite,
Point out the game, and animate the flight;
That from Marseilles to Calais, France may know,
As we have conquerors, we have poets too;
And either laurel does in Britain grow;
That, though amongst ourselves, with too much
heat,
We sometimes wrangle, when we should debate;
(A consequential ill which freedom draws;
A bad effect, but from a noble cause);
We can with universal zeal advance,
To curb the faithless arrogance of France;
Nor ever shall Britannia's sons refuse
To answer to thy master or thy muse;
Nor want just subject for victorious strains;
While Marlborough's arm eternal laurels gain;
And where old Spenser sung, a new Eliza reigns.

FOR THE PLAN OF A FOUNTAIN,

On which are the Effigies of the Queen on a Triumphal Arch, the Duke of Marlborough beneath, and the chief Rivers of the World round the whole Work.

Ye active streams, where'er your waters flow,
Let distant climes and furthest nations know,
What ye from Thames and Danube have been taught,
How Anne commanded, and how Marlborough fought.

Quacunque æterno properatis, flumina, lapsu,
Divisis latè terris, populisque remotis,
Dicite, nam vobis Tamisis narravit et Ister,
Anna quid imperiis potuit, quid Marlburus armis.

THE CHAMELEON.

As the Chameleon, who is known
To have no colors of his own :
But borrows from his neighbour's hue
His white or black, his green or blue ;
And struts as much in ready light,
Which credit gives him upon sight :

As if the rainbow were in tail
Settled on him, and his heirs male;
So the young squire, when first he comes
From country school to Will's or Tom's:[1]
And equally, in truth is fit
To be a statesman or a wit;
Without one notion of his own,
He saunters wildly up and down;
Till some acquaintance, good or bad,
Takes notice of a staring lad;
Admits him in among the gang:
They jest, reply, dispute, harangue;
He acts and talks, as they befriend him,
Smear'd with the colours which they lend him.
  Thus merely, as his fortune chances,
His merit or his vice advances.
  If haply he the sect pursues,
That read and comment upon news;
He takes up their mysterious face:
He drinks his coffee without lace.
This week his mimic-tongue runs o'er
What they have said the week before;
His wisdom sets all Europe right,
And teaches Marborough when to fight.
  Or if it be his fate to meet
With folks who have more wealth than wit;
He loves cheap port, and double bub;
And settles in the hum-drum club:

[1] Two celebrated coffee-houses.

He learns how stocks will fall or rise;
Holds poverty the greatest vice;
Thinks wit the bane of conversation;
And says that learning spoils a nation.
  But if, at first, he minds his hits,
And drinks champagne among the wits!
Five deep he toasts the towering lasses;
Repeats you verses wrote on glasses;
Is in the chair; prescribes the law;
And lies with those he never saw.

MERRY ANDREW.

Sly Merry Andrew, the last Southwark fair
(At Barthol'mew he did not much appear:
So peevish was the edict of the Mayor)
At Southwark therefore as his tricks he show'd,
To please our masters, and his friends the crowd;
A huge neat's tongue he in his right hand held:
His left was with a good black pudding fill'd.
With a grave look in this odd equipage,
The clownish mimic traverses the stage:
Why how now, Andrew! cries his brother droll,
To-day's conceit, methinks, is something dull:
Come on, Sir, to our worthy friends explain,
What does your emblematic worship mean?
Quoth Andrew; Honest English let us speak:

Your emble—(what d'ye call't) is heathen Greek.
To tongue or pudding thou hast no pretence:
Learning thy talent is, but mine is sense.
That busy fool I was, which thou art now;
Desirous to correct, not knowing how:
With very good design, but little wit,
Blaming or praising things, as I thought fit.
I for this conduct had what I deserv'd;
And dealing honestly, was almost starv'd.
But, thanks to my indulgent stars, I eat;
Since I have found the secret to be great.
O, dearest Andrew, says the humble droll,
Henceforth may I obey, and thou control;
Provided thou impart thy useful skill.—
Bow then, says Andrew; and, for once, I will.—
Be of your patron's mind, whate'er he says;
Sleep very much; think little; and talk less;
Mind neither good nor bad, nor right nor wrong,
But eat your pudding, slave; and hold your tongue.

A reverend prelate stopp'd his coach and six,
To laugh a little at our Andrew's tricks;
But when he heard him give this golden rule,
Drive on (he cried); this fellow is no fool.

A SIMILE.

Dear Thomas, didst thou never pop
Thy head into a tin-man's shop?
There, Thomas, didst thou never see
('Tis but by way of simile)
A squirrel spend his little rage,
In jumping round a rolling cage?
The cage, as either side turn'd up,
Striking a ring of bells a-top?—
  Mov'd in the orb, pleas'd with the chimes,
The foolish creature thinks he climbs:
But here or there, turn wood or wire,
He never gets two inches higher.
  So fares it with those merry blades,
That frisk it under Pindus' shades.
In noble songs, and lofty odes,
They tread on stars, and talk with gods;
Still dancing in an airy round,
Still pleas'd with their own verses' sound;
Brought back, how fast soe'er they go,
Always aspiring, always low.

THE FLIES.

SAY, sire of insects, mighty Sol,
(A Fly upon the chariot pole
Cries out) what Blue-bottle alive
Did ever with such fury drive?
Tell Belzebub, great father, tell,
(Says t'other, perch'd upon the wheel)
Did ever any mortal Fly
Raise such a cloud of dust as I?
   My judgment turn'd the whole debate:
My valour sav'd the sinking state.
So talk two idle buzzing things;
Toss up their heads, and stretch their wings.
But let the truth to light be brought:
This neither spoke, nor t'other fought:
No merit in their own behaviour:
Both rais'd, but by their party's favour.

A PARAPHRASE FROM THE FRENCH.

IN grey-hair'd Celia's wither'd arms
   As mighty Lewis lay,
She cried, "If I have any charms,
   My dearest, let's away!

For you, my love, is all my fear,
  Hark how the drums do rattle;
Alas, sir! what should you do here
  In dreadful day of battle?
Let little Orange stay and fight,
  For danger's his diversion;
The wise will think you in the right,
  Not to expose your person:
Nor vex your thoughts how to repair
  The ruins of your glory;
You ought to leave so mean a care
  To those who pen your story.
Are not Boileau and Corneille paid
  For panegyric writing?
They know how heroes may be made
  Without the help of fighting.
When foes too saucily approach,
  'Tis best to leave them fairly;
Put six good horses in your coach,
  And carry me to Marly.
Let Boufleurs, to secure your fame,
  Go take some town, or buy it;
Whilst you, great sir, at Nostredame,
  Te Deum sing in quiet!"

FROM THE GREEK.

GREAT Bacchus, born in thunder and in fire,
By native heat asserts his dreadful sire.
Nourish'd near shady rills and cooling streams,
He to the nymphs avows his amorous flames.
To all the brethren at the Bell and Vine,
The moral says; mix water with your wine.

EPIGRAM.

FRANK carves very ill, yet will palm all the meats:
He eats more than six; and drinks more than he eats.
Four pipes after dinner he constantly smokes;
And seasons his whiffs with impertinent jokes.
Yet sighing, he says, we must certainly break;
And my cruel unkindness compels him to speak;
For of late I invite him—but four times a week.

ANOTHER.

To John I ow'd great obligation;
But John unhappily thought fit
To publish it to all the nation:
Sure John and I are more than quit.

ANOTHER.

Yes, every poet is a fool:
By demonstration Ned can show it:
Happy, could Ned's inverted rule
Prove every fool to be a poet.

ANOTHER.

Thy nags, (the leanest things alive)
So very hard thou lov'st to drive;
I heard thy anxious coachman say,
It cost thee more in whips than hay.

TO A PERSON WHO WROTE ILL, AND SPOKE WORSE AGAINST ME.

Lie, Philo, untouch'd on my peaceable shelf;
Nor take it amiss, that so little I heed thee:
I've no envy to thee, and some love to myself:
Then why should I answer; since first I must read thee?

Drunk with Helicon's waters and double-brew'd bub,
Be a linguist, a poet, a critic, a wag;

To the solid delight of thy well-judging club,
 To the damage alone of thy bookseller Brag.

Pursue me with satire: what harm is there in't?
 But from all viva voce reflection forbear:
There can be no danger from what thou shalt print:
 There may be a little from what thou may'st swear.

ON THE SAME PERSON.

While, faster than his costive brain indites,
Philo's quick hand in flowing letters writes;
His case appears to me like honest Teague's,
When he was run away with, by his legs.
Phœbus, give Philo o'er himself command;
Quicken his senses, or restrain his hand;
Let him be kept from paper, pen, and ink:
So may he cease to write, and learn to think.

"QUID SIT FUTURUM CRAS FUGE QUÆRERE."

For what to-morrow shall disclose,
May spoil what you to-night propose:
England may change; or Cloe stray:
Love and life are for to-day.

A BALLAD OF THE NOTBROWNE MAYDE.[1]

A.

Be it ryght, or wrong, these men among on women
do complayne ;
Affyrmynge this—how that it is a labour spent in
vayne,

[1] This ancient poem was originally printed in an old black-letter book, entitled, The Customes of London or Arnolde's Chronicle, which Mr. Capell supposes appeared about the year 1521. According to that gentleman's opinion—"It was certainly written in the beginning of the sixteenth century, and not sooner: the curious in these matters, who shall conceive a doubt of what is here asserted through remembrance of what he has seen advanced by a poet of late days, is desired to look into the works of the great Sir Thomas More, and particularly into a poem that stands at the head of them, and from thence receive conviction; if sameness of rhymes, sameness of orthography, and a very near affinity of words and phrases be capable of giving it." The poet of late days mentioned above, is certainly Mr. Prior, who in the edition of his poems published in 1718, had asserted it to have been written three hundred years since. What led him to that mistaken notion, was probably a writer in the Muses Mercury for June 1707, who conjectures that it was written about the year 1472. The same writer says, and the ballad seems to confirm it, that the persons represented are a young Lord, the Earl of Westmoreland's son, and a lady of equal quality. The copy from which this poem hath hitherto been printed being very inaccurate, it is here given according to that published by Mr. Capell.

To love them wele; for never a dele they love a
man agayne:
For late a man do what he can, theyr favour to
attayne,
Yet, yf a newe do them pursue, theyr fyrst true
lover than
Laboureth for nought; for from her thought he is
a banyshed man.

B.

I say nat, nay, but that all day it is bothe writ and
sayd,
That womens fayth is, as who sayth, all utterly
decayed:
But, neverthelesse, ryght good wytnèsse in this
case might be layed,
That they love true, and continùe; recorde the not-
browne mayde;
Which, when her love came, her to prove, to her to
make his mone,
Wolde nat depart; for in her hart she loved but
hym alone.

A.

Than betwayne us late us dyscus what was all the
manère
Betwayne them two: we wyll also tell all the payne,
and fere,
That she was in: nowe I begyn, so that ye me an-
swère;—
Wherefore, all ye, that present be, I pray you give
an ere:—

I am the knyght; I come by nyght, as secret as I
can;
Sayinge, Alas, thus standeth the case, I am a banyshed man.

B.

And I your wyll for to fulfyll in this wyll nat refuse;
Trustynge to shewe in wordes fewe, that men have
na yll use
(To theyr own shame) women to blame, and causelesse them accuse:
Therfore to you I answere nowe, all women to excuse,—
Myne owne hart dere, with you what chere? I pray
you, tell anone;
For, in my mynde, of all mankynde I love but you
alone.

A.

It standeth so; a dede is do, whereof grete harme
shall growe:
My destiny is for to dy a shamefull deth, I trowe;
Or elles to fle: the one must be; none other way
I knowe,
But to withdrawe as an outlawe, and take me to
my bowe.
Wherfore, adue, my owne hart true! none other
rede I can;
For I must to the grene wode go, alone, a banyshed
man.

B.

O Lorde, what is this worldys blysse, that chaungeth as the mone!
The somers day in lusty May is derked before the none.—
I here you say, farewell; nay, nay, we départ nat so sone:
Why say ye so? wheder wyll ye go? alas, what have ye done?
All my welfàre to sorrowe and care sholde chaunge, yf ye were gone;
For, in my mynde, of all mankynde I love but you alone.

A.

I can beleve, it shall you greve, and somwhat you dystrayne:
But, aftyrwarde, your paynes harde within a day or twayne
Shall sone aslake; and ye shall take comfort to you agayne.
Why sholde ye ought? for, to make thought, your labour were in vayne.
And thus I do; and pray you to, as hartely as I can;
For I must to the grene wode go, alone, a banyshed man.

B.

Now, syth that ye have shewed to me the secret of your mynde,
I shall be playne to you agayne, lyke as ye shall me fynde:

Syth it is so that ye wyll go, I wolle not leve behynde;
Shall it never be sayd, the Notbrowne mayd was to her love unkynde: [anone;
Make you redy; for so am I, although it were
For, in my mynde, of all mankynde I love but you alone.

A.

Yet I you rede to take good hede what men wyll thynke and say:
Of younge and olde it shall be tolde, that ye be gone away;
Your wanton wyll for to fulfill, in grene wode you to play;
And that ye myght from your delyght no lenger make delay:
Rather than ye sholde thus for me be called an yll womàn,
Yet wolde I to the grene wode go, alone, a banyshed man.

B.

Though it be songe of olde and yonge, that I sholde be to blame,
Theyrs be the charge that speke so large in hurtynge of my name:
For I wyll prove, that faythful love it is devoyd of shame;
In your dystresse, and hevynesse, to part wyth you, the same;
To shewe all tho that do nat so, true lovers are they none:

For, in my mynde, of all mankynde I love but you alone.

A.

I counceyle you, remember howe it is no mayden's lawe,
Nothynge to dout, but to renne out to wode with an outlàwe:
For ye must there in your hand bere a bowe, redy to drawe;
And, as a thefe, thus must you lyve, ever in drede and awe;
Whereby to you grete harme myght growe: yet had I lever than,
That I had to the grene wode go, alone, a banyshed man.

B.

I say nat, nay, but as ye say, it is no mayden's lore:
But love may make me, for your sake, as I have sayd before,
To come on fote, to hunt, and shote, to get us mete in store;
For so that I your company may have, I aske no more:
From which to part, it maketh my hart as colde as ony stone;
For, in my mynde, of all mankynde I love but you alone.

A.

For an outlawe, this is the lawe,—that men hym take and bynde;

Without pytè, hanged to be, and waver with the wynde.
Yf I had nede, (as God forbede!) what socours coude ye fynde?
For sothe I trowe, ye and your bowe for fere wolde drawe behynde:
And no mervayle; for lytell avayle were in your counceyle than:
Wherfore I'll to the grene wode go, alone, a banyshed man.

B.

Ryght wele know ye, that women be but feble for to fyght;
No womanhede it is, indede, to be bolde as a knyght:
Yet, in such fere yf that ye were with enemyes day and nyght,
I wolde withstande, with bowe in hande, to helpe you with my myght,
And you to save; as women have from deth many a one;
For, in my mynde, of all mankynde I love but you alone.

A.

Yet take good hede; for ever I drede that ye coude nat sustayne
The thornie wayes, the depe valèies, the snowe, the frost, the rayne,
The colde, the hete: for, drye, or wete, we must lodge on the playne;
And, us above, none other rofe but a brake, bush, or twayne:

Which sone sholde greve you, I beleve; and ye wolde gladly than
That I had to the grene wode go, a lone, a banyshed man.

B.

Syth I have here been partynère with you of joy and blysse,
I must also parte of your wo endure, as reson is:
Yet am I sure of one plesùre; and shortely, it is this,—
That, where ye be, me semeth, pardè, I coude not fare amysse.
Without more speche, I you beseche that we were shortely gone;
For, in my mynde, of all mankynde I love but you alone.

A.

Yf ye go thyder, ye must consider,—whan ye have lust to dyne,
There shall no mete, be for to gete, neyther bere, ale, ne wyne;
Ne shetes clene to lye betwene, maden of threde and twyne;
None other house, but leves and bowes, to cover your hed and myne:
O myne hart swete, this evyll dyète sholde make you pale and wan;
Wherfore I'll to the grene wode go, alone, a banyshed man;

B.

Amonge the wylde dere, such an archère as men
say that ye be,
May ye nat fayle of good vitayle, where is so grete
plentè ?
And water clere of the ryvère shall be full swete to
me ;
With which in hele I shall ryght wele endure, as
ye shall see :
And, or we go, a bedde or two I can provyde anone ;
For, in my mynde, of all mankynde I love but you
alone.

A.

Lo yet, before, ye must do more, yf ye wyll go with
me:
As cut your here above your ere, your kyrtel above
the kne ;
With bowe in hande, for to withstande your ene-
myes, yf nede be :
And, this same nyght, before day-lyght, to wode-
warde wyll I fle.
Yf that ye wyll all this fulfill, do it shortely as ye
can ;
Els wyll I to the grene wode go, alone, a banyshed
man.

B.

I shall as nowe do more for you than longeth to
womanhede ;
To shorte my here, a bow to bere, to shote in tyme
of nede :—

O my swete mother, before all other for you I have most drede :
But nowe, adue ! I must ensue where fortune doth me lede.—
All this make ye : nowe let us fle ; the day cometh fast upon ;
For, in my mynde, of all mankynde I love but you alone.

A.

Nay, nay, nat so ; ye shal nat go, and I shall tell you why,—
Your appetyght is to be lyght of love, I wele espy :
For, lyke as ye have sayed to me, in lyke wyse hardely
Ye wolde answère, whosoever it were, in way of company.
It is sayd of olde,—Sone hote, sone colde ; and so is a womàn :
For I must to the grene wode go, alone, a banyshed man.

B.

Yf ye take hede, it is no nede such wordes to say by me :
For oft ye prayed, and long assayed, or I you loved, pardè :
And though that I of auncestry a baron's daughter be,
Yet have you proved howe I you loved, a squyer of lowe degre ;
And ever shall, whatso befall ; to dye therefore anone ;

For, in my mynde, of all mankynde I love but you alone.

A.

A baron's chylde to be begylde! it were a cursed dede:
To be felàwe with an outlàwe! Almighty God forbede!
Yea, beter were, the pore squyère alone to forest yede,
Than ye sholde say another day, that by my cursed dede
Ye were betrayed: wherfore, good mayd, the best rede that I can,
Is, that I to the green wode go, alone, a banyshed man.

B.

Whatever befall, I never shall of this thyng you upbrayd:
But yf ye go, and leve me so, than have ye me betrayed.
Remember you wele howe that ye dele; for, yf ye be as ye sayd,
Ye were unkynde, to leue behynde, your love, the notbrowne mayd.
Trust me truly, that I shall dy sone after ye be gone;
For, in my mynde, of all maukynde I love but you alone.

A.

Yf that ye went, ye sholde repent; for in the forest nowe

I have purvayed me of a mayd, whom I love more than you;
Another fayrère than ever ye were, I dare it wele avowe;
And of you bothe eche sholde be wrothe with other, as I trowe:
It were myne ese, to lyve in pese; so wyll I, yf I can;
Wherfore I to the grene wode go, alone, a banyshed man.

B.

Though in the wode I undyrstode ye had a paramour,
All this may nought remove my thought, but that I will be your:
And she shall fynde me soft, and kynde, and courteys every hour;
Glad to fulfyll all that she wyll commaunde me, to my power:
For had ye, lo, an hundred mo, yet wolde I be that one;
For, in my mynde, of all mankynde I love but you alone.

A.

Myne own dere love, I se the prove that ye be kynde, and true;
Of mayde, and wyfe, in all my lyfe, the best that ever I knewe.
Be mery and glad, be no more sad, the case is chaunged newe;

For it were ruthe, that, for your truthe, ye sholde
have cause to rewe:
Be nat dismayed; whatsoever I sayd to you, whan
I began,
I will nat to the grene wode go, I am no banyshed
man.

B.

These tydings be more gladder to me than to be
made a quene,
Yf I were sure they sholde endure: but it is often
sene,
Whan men wyll breke promyse, they speke the
wordes on the splene:
Ye shape some wyle, me to begyle, and stele from
me, I wene:
Than were the case worse than it was, and I more
wo-begone;
For, in my mynde, of all mankynde I love but you
alone.

A.

Ye shall nat nede further to drede; I wyll not dys-
parage
You (God defende!) syth you descend of so grete
lynage.
Nowe understande,—to Westmarlande, which is
myne herytage,
I wyll you bringe; and with a rynge, by way of
maryage
I wyll you take, and lady make, as shortely as I
can:

Thus have ye won an erlys son, and not a banyshed
man.

B.

Here may ye se, that women be, in love, meke,
kynde, and stable:
Late never man reprove them than, ...
But, rather, pray God, that we may to them be
comfortable,
Which sometyme proved such as he loved, yf they
be charytable.
Forsoth, men wolde that women sholde be meke to
them eche one;
Moche more ought they to God obey, and serve
but hym alone.

HENRY AND EMMA. A POEM.

UPON THE MODEL OF THE NUT-BROWN MAID.

TO CLOE.

Thou, to whose eyes I bend, at whose command
(Though low my voice, though artless be my hand)
I take the sprightly reed, and sing, and play;
Careless of what the censuring world may say:
Bright Cloe, object of my constant vow,
Wilt thou awhile unbend thy serious brow;
Wilt thou with pleasure hear thy lover's strains,
And with one heavenly smile o'erpay his pains?

No longer shall the Nut-brown Maid be old;
Though since her youth three hundred years have [roll'd:
At thy desire she shall again be raised;
And her reviving charms in lasting verse be prais'd.
  No longer man of woman shall complain,
That he may love, and not be lov'd again:
That we in vain the fickle sex pursue,
Who change the constant lover for the new.
Whatever has been writ, whatever said,
Of female passion feign'd or faith decay'd:
Henceforth shall in my verse refuted stand,
Be said to winds, or writ upon the sand.
And, while my notes to future times proclaim
Unconquer'd love, and ever-during flame;
O fairest of the sex! be thou my Muse:
Deign on my work thy influence to diffuse.
Let me partake the blessings I rehearse,
And grant me, love, the just reward of verse!
  As beauty's potent queen, with every grace
That once was Emma's, has adorn'd thy face;
And as her son has to my bosom dealt
That constant flame, which faithful Henry felt;
O let the story with thy life agree:
Let men once more the bright example see;
What Emma was to him, be thou to me.
Nor send me by thy frown from her I love,
Distant and sad, a banish'd man to rove.
But oh! with pity, long-entreated, crown
My pains and hopes; and when thou say'st that one
Of all mankind thou lov'st, oh! think on me alone.

Where beauteous Isis and her husband Tame
With mingled waves for ever flow the same,
In times of yore an ancient baron liv'd;
Great gifts bestow'd, and great respect receiv'd.
When dreadful Edward with successful care
Led his free Britons to the Gallic war;
This lord had headed his appointed bands,
In firm allegiance to his king's commands;
And (all due honours faithfully discharg'd)
Had brought back his paternal coat enlarg'd
With a new mark, the witness of his toil,
And no inglorious part of foreign spoil.
From the loud camp retir'd and noisy court,
In honourable ease and rural sport,
The remnant of his days he safely pass'd;
Nor found they lagg'd too slow, nor flew too fast.
He made his wish with his estate comply,
Joyful to live, yet not afraid to die.
One child he had, a daughter chaste and fair,
His age's comfort, and his fortune's heir.
They call'd her Emma; for the beauteous dame,
Who gave the virgin birth, had borne the name;
The name th' indulgent father doubly lov'd;
For in the child the mother's charms improv'd.
Yet as, when little, round his knees she play'd,
He call'd her oft in sport his Nut-brown Maid,
The friends and tenants took the fondling word
(As still they please, who imitate their lord);
Usage confirm'd what fancy had begun;
The mutual terms around the lands were known;

And Emma and the Nut-brown Maid were one.
As with her stature, still her charms increas'd;
Through all the isle her beauty was confess'd.
Oh! what perfection must that virgin share,
Who fairest is esteem'd, where all are fair!
From distant shires repair the noble youth,
And find report for once had lessen'd truth.
By wonder first, and then by passion mov'd,
They came; they saw; they marvell'd; and they lov'd.
By public praises, and by secret sighs,
Each own'd the general power of Emma's eyes.
In tilts and tournaments the valiant strove,
By glorious deeds to purchase Emma's love.
In gentle verse the witty told their flame,
And grac'd their choicest songs with Emma's name.
In vain they combated, in vain they writ:
Useless their strength, and impotent their wit.
Great Venus only must direct the dart,
Which else will never reach the fair one's heart,
Spite of th' attempts of force, and soft effects of art.
Great Venus must prefer the happy one:
In Henry's cause her favour must be shown:
And Emma, of mankind, must love but him alone.
While these in public to the castle came,
And by their grandeur justified their flame;
More secret ways the careful Henry takes;
His squires, his arms, and equipage forsakes:

In borrow'd name and false attire array'd,
Oft he finds means to see the beauteous maid.
When Emma hunts, in huntsman's habit drest,
Henry on foot pursues the bounding beast.
In his right hand his beechen pole he bears:
And graceful at his side his horn he wears.
Still to the glade, where she has bent her way,
With knowing skill he drives the future prey;
Bids her decline the hill, and shun the brake;
And shews the path her steed may safest take;
Directs her spear to fix the glorious wound;
Pleas'd in his toils to have her triumph crown'd;
And blows her praises in no common sound.
A falconer Henry is, when Emma hawks:
With her of tarsels and of lures he talks.
Upon his wrist the towering merlin stands,
Practis'd to rise, and stoop at her commands.
And when superior now the bird has flown,
And headlong brought the tumbling quarry down;
With humble reverence he accosts the fair,
And with the honour'd feather decks her hair.
Yet still, as from the sportive field she goes,
His downcast eye reveals his inward woes;
And by his look and sorrow is express'd,
A nobler game pursued than bird or beast.
A shepherd now along the plain he roves;
And, with his jolly pipe, delights the groves.
The neighbouring swains around the stranger throng,
Or to admire, or emulate his song:

While with soft sorrow he renews his lays,
Nor heedful of their envy, nor their praise.
But, soon as Emma's eyes adorn the plain,
His notes he raises to a nobler strain,
With dutiful respect, and studious fear;
Lest any careless sound offend her ear.
A frantic gipsy now, the house he haunts,
And in wild phrases speaks dissembled wants.
With the fond maids in palmistry he deals:
They tell the secret first, which he reveals;
Says who shall wed, and who shall be beguil'd;
What groom shall get, and 'squire maintain the child.
But, when bright Emma would her fortune know,
A softer look unbends his opening brow;
With trembling awe he gazes on her eye,
And in soft accents forms the kind reply;
That she shall prove as fortunate as fair;
And Hymen's choicest gifts are all reserv'd for her.
Now oft had Henry chang'd his sly disguise,
Unmark'd by all but beauteous Emma's eyes;
Oft had found means alone to see the dame,
And at her feet to breathe his amorous flame;
And oft the pangs of absence to remove
By letters, soft interpreters of love:
Till Time and Industry (the mighty two
That bring our wishes nearer to our view)
Made him perceive, that the inclining fair
Receiv'd his vows with no reluctant ear;
That Venus had confirm'd her equal reign,

And dealt to Emma's heart a share of Henry's pain.
While Cupid smil'd, by kind occasion bless'd,
And, with the secret kept, the love increas'd;
The amorous youth frequents the silent groves;
And much he meditates, for much he loves.
He loves: 'tis true; and is beloved again:
Great are his joys: but will they long remain?
Emma with smiles receives his present flame;
But smiling, will she ever be the same?
Beautiful looks are ruled by fickle minds;
And summer seas are turn'd by sudden winds.
Another love may gain her easy youth:
Time changes thought; and flattery conquers truth.
O impotent estate of human life!
Where hope and fear maintain eternal strife!
Where fleeting joy does lasting doubt inspire;
And most we question what we most desire!
Amongst thy various gifts, great Heaven, bestow
Our cup of love unmix'd; forbear to throw
Bitter ingredients in; nor pall the draught
With nauseous grief: for our ill-judging thought
Hardly enjoys the pleasurable taste;
Or deems it not sincere; or fears it cannot last.
With wishes rais'd, with jealousies opprest,
(Alternate tyrants of the human breast)
By one great trial he resolves to prove
The faith of woman, and the force of love.
If scanning Emma's virtues he may find
That beauteous frame enclose a steady mind,
He'll fix his hope, of future joy secure,

And live a slave to Hymen's happy power.
But if the fair one, as he fears, is frail;
If, pois'd aright in reason's equal scale,
Light fly her merit, and her faults prevail;
His mind he vows to free from amorous care,
The latent mischief from his heart to tear,
Resume his azure arms, and shine again in war.
South of the castle, in a verdant glade,
A spreading beech extends her friendly shade:
Here oft the nymph his breathing vows had heard;
Here oft her silence had her heart declar'd.
As active spring awak'd her infant buds,
And genial life inform'd the verdant woods;
Henry in knots involving Emma's name,
Had half express'd and half conceal'd his flame,
Upon this tree: and, as the tender mark
Grew with the year, and widn'd with the bark,
Venus had heard the virgin's soft address,
That, as the wound, the passion might increase.
As potent Nature shed her kindly showers,
And deck'd the various mead with opening flowers;
Upon this tree the nymph's obliging care
Had left a frequent wreath for Henry's hair;
Which as with gay delight the lover found,
Pleas'd with his conquest, with her present crown'd,
Glorious through all the plains he oft had gone,
And to each swain the mystic honour shown;
The gift still prais'd, the giver still unknown.
His secret note the troubled Henry writes;
To the known tree the lovely maid invites:

Imperfect words and dubious terms express,
That unforeseen mischance disturb'd his peace;
That he must something to her ear commend,
On which her conduct and his life depend.
  Soon as the fair one had the note receiv'd,
The remnant of the day alone she griev'd:
For different this from every former note,
Which Venus dictated, and Henry wrote;
Which told her all his future hopes were laid
On the dear bosom of his Nut-brown Maid;
Which always bless'd her eyes, and own'd her power,
And bid her oft adieu, yet added more.
Now night advanced. The house in sleep were laid:
The nurse experienc'd, and the prying maid;
At last that sprite, which does incessant haunt
The lover's steps, the ancient maiden-aunt.
To her dear Henry Emma wings her way,
With quicken'd pace repairing forc'd delay;
For love, fantastic power, that is afraid
To stir abroad till watchfulness be laid,
Undaunted then o'er cliffs and valleys strays,
And leads his votaries safe through pathless ways.
Not Argus with his hundred eyes shall find
Where Cupid goes: though he, poor guide! is
blind.
  The maiden first arriving, sent her eye
To ask, if yet its chief delight were nigh:
With fear and with desire, with joy and pain,
She sees, and runs to meet him on the plain.
But oh! his steps proclaim no lover's haste:

On the low ground his fix'd regards are cast;
His artful bosom heaves dissembled sighs;
And tears suborn'd fall copious from his eyes.
With ease, alas! we credit what we love:
His painted grief does real sorrow move
In the afflicted fair; adown her cheek
Trickling the genuine tears their current break;
Attentive stood the mournful nymph: the man
Broke silence first: the tale alternate ran.

HENRY.

Sincere, O tell me, hast thou felt a pain,
Emma, beyond what woman knows to feign?
Has thy uncertain bosom ever strove
With the first tumults of a real love?
Hast thou now dreaded, and now blest his sway,
By turns averse, and joyful to obey?
Thy virgin softness hast thou e'er bewail'd;
As Reason yielded, and as Love prevail'd?
And wept the potent god's resistless dart,
His killing pleasure, his ecstatic smart,
And heavenly poison thrilling through thy heart?
If so, with pity view my wretched state;
At least deplore, and then forget my fate:
To some more happy knight reserve thy charms;
By Fortune favour'd, and successful arms:
And only, as the sun's revolving ray
Brings back each year this melancholy day,
Permit one sigh, and set apart one tear,
To an abandon'd exile's endless care.

For me, alas! outcast of human race,
Love's anger only waits, and dire disgrace;
For lo! these hands in murther are imbrued;
These trembling feet by justice are pursued:
Fate calls aloud, and hastens me away;
A shameful death attends my longer stay;
And I this night must fly from thee and love,
Condemn'd in lonely woods, a banish'd man, to
rove.

EMMA.

What is our bliss, that changeth with the moon;
And day of life, that darkens ere 'tis noon?
What is true passion, if unblest it dies?
And where is Emma's joy, if Henry flies?
If love, alas! be pain; the pain I bear
No thought can figure, and no tongue declare.
Ne'er faithful woman felt, nor false one feign'd,
The flames which long have in my bosom reign'd:
The god of love himself inhabits there,
With all his rage, and dread, and grief, and care,
His complement of stores, and total war.
O! cease then coldly to suspect my love;
And let my deed at least my faith approve.
Alas! no youth shall my endearments share;
Nor day nor night shall interrupt my care;
No future story shall with truth upbraid
The cold indifference of the Nut-brown Maid:
Nor to hard banishment shall Henry run,
While careless Emma sleeps on beds of down.
View me resolv'd, where'er thou leadst, to go,

Friend to thy pain, and partner of thy woe;
For I attest fair Venus and her son,
That I, of all mankind, will love but thee alone.

HENRY.

Let prudence yet obstruct thy venturous way;
And take good heed, what men will think and say:
That beauteous Emma vagrant courses took;
Her father's house and civil life forsook;
That, full of youthful blood, and fond of man,
She to the woodland with an exile ran.
Reflect, that lessen'd fame is ne'er regain'd;
And virgin honour, once, is always stain'd:
Timely advis'd, the coming evil shun:
Better not do the deed, than weep it done.
No penance can absolve our guilty fame;
Nor tears, that wash out sin, can wash out shame.
Then fly the sad effects of desperate love:
And leave a banish'd man through lonely woods to rove.

EMMA.

Let Emma's hapless case be falsely told
By the rash young, or the ill-natur'd old:
Let every tongue its various censures choose;
Absolve with coldness, or with spite accuse:
Fair truth at last her radiant beams will raise;
And malice vanquish'd heightens virtue's praise.
Let then thy favour but indulge my flight;
O! let my presence make thy travels light;

And potent Venus shall exalt my name,
Above the rumours of censorious Fame;
Nor from that busy demon's restless power
Will ever Emma other grace implore,
Than that this truth should to the world be known,
That I, of all mankind, have lov'd but thee alone.

HENRY.

But canst thou wield the sword, and bend the bow?
With active force repel the sturdy foe?
When the loud tumult speaks the battle nigh,
And winged deaths in whistling arrows fly;
Wilt thou, though wounded, yet undaunted stay,
Perform thy part, and share the dangerous day?
Then, as thy strength decays, thy heart will fail,
Thy limbs all trembling, and thy cheeks all pale;
With fruitless sorrow, thou, inglorious maid,
Wilt weep thy safety by thy love betray'd:
Then to thy friend, by foes o'ercharg'd, deny
Thy little useless aid, and coward fly:
Then wilt thou curse the chance that made thee love
A banish'd man, condemn'd in lonely woods to rove.

EMMA.

With fatal certainty Thalestris knew
To send the arrow from the twanging yew;
And, great in arms, and foremost in the war,
Bonduca brandish'd high the British spear.
Could thirst of vengeance and desire of fame
Excite the female breast with martial flame?

And shall not love's diviner power inspire
More hardy virtue, and more generous fire?
Near thee, mistrust not, constant I'll abide,
And fall, or vanquish, fighting by thy side.
Though my inferior strength may not allow,
That I should bear or draw the warrior bow;
With ready hand, I will the shaft supply,
And joy to see thy victor arrows fly.
Touch'd in the battle by the hostile reed,
Shouldst thou (but heaven avert it!) shouldst thou bleed;
To stop the wounds, my finest lawn I'd tear,
Wash them with tears, and wipe them with my hair;
Blest, when my dangers and my toils have shown
That I, of all mankind, could love but thee alone.

HENRY.

But canst thou, tender maid, canst thou sustain
Afflictive want, or hunger's pressing pain?
Those limbs, in lawn and softest silk array'd,
From sunbeams guarded, and of winds afraid;
Can they bear angry Jove? can they resist
The parching dog-star, and the bleak north-east?
When, chill'd by adverse snows and beating rain,
We tread with weary steps the longsome plain;
When with hard toil we seek our evening food,
Berries and acorns, from the neighbouring wood;
And find among the cliffs no other house,
But the thin covert of some gathered boughs
Wilt thou not then reluctant send thine eye
Around the dreary waste; and weeping try

(Though then, alas! that trial be too late)
To find thy father's hospitable gate,
And seats, where ease and plenty brooding sate?
Those seats, whence long excluded thou must
mourn;
That gate, for ever barr'd to thy return:
Wilt thou not then bewail ill-fated love,
And hate a banish'd man, condemn'd in woods to
rove?

EMMA.

Thy rise of fortune did I only wed,
From its decline determin'd to recede;
Did I but purpose to embark with thee
On the smooth surface of a summer's sea;
While gentle zephyrs play in prosperous gales,
And fortune's favour fills the swelling sails;
But would forsake the ship, and make the shore,
When the winds whistle, and the tempests roar?
No, Henry, no: one sacred oath has tied
Our loves; one destiny our life shall guide;
Nor wild nor deep our common way divide.
When from the cave thou risest with the day,
To beat the woods, and rouse the bounding prey;
The cave with moss and branches I'll adorn,
And cheerful sit, to wait my lord's return:
And, when thou frequent bringst the smitten deer
(For seldom, archers say, thy arrows err),
I'll fetch quick fuel from the neighbouring wood,
And strike the sparkling flint, and dress the food;
With humble duty and officious haste,

I'll cull the furthest mead for thy repast;
The choicest herbs I to thy board will bring,
And draw thy water from the freshest spring:
And, when at night with weary toil opprest,
Soft slumbers thou enjoy'st, and wholesome rest;
Watchful I'll guard thee, and with midnight prayer
Weary the gods to keep thee in their care;
And joyous ask, at morn's returning ray,
If thou hast health, and I may bless the day.
My thoughts shall fix, my latest wish depend,
On thee, guide, guardian, kinsman, father, friend
By all these sacred names be Henry known
To Emma's heart; and grateful let him own,
That she, of all mankind, could love but him alone

HENRY.

Vainly thou tell'st me, what the woman's care
Shall in the wildness of the wood prepare:
Thou, ere thou goest, unhappiest of thy kind,
Must leave the habit and the sex behind.
No longer shall thy comely tresses break
In flowing ringlets on thy snowy neck;
Or sit behind thy head, an ample round,
In graceful braids with various ribbon bound:
No longer shall the bodice, aptly lac'd,
From thy full bosom to thy slender waist,
That air and harmony of shape express,
Fine by degrees, and beautifully less:
Nor shall thy lower garments artful plait,
From thy fair side dependent to thy feet,

Arm their chaste beauties with a modest pride,
And double every charm they seek to hide.
Th' ambrosial plenty of thy shining hair,
Cropt off and lost, scarce lower than thy ear
Shall stand uncouth: a horseman's coat shall hide
Thy taper shape, and comeliness of side:
The short trunk-hose shall show thy foot and knee
Licentious, and to common eye-sight free:
And, with a bolder stride and looser air,
Mingled with men, a man thou must appear.
Nor solitude, nor gentle peace of mind,
Mistaken maid, shalt thou in forests find:
'Tis long since Cynthia and her train were there:
Or guardian gods made innocence their care.
Vagrants and outlaws shall offend thy view:
For such must be my friends, a hideous crew.
By adverse fortune mix'd in social ill,
Train'd to assault, and disciplin'd to kill:
Their common loves, a lewd abandon'd pack,
The beadle's lash still flagrant on their back:
By sloth corrupted, by disorder fed,
Made bold by want, and prostitute for bread:
With such must Emma hunt the tedious day,
Assist their violence, and divide their prey:
With such she must return at setting light,
Though not partaker, witness of their night.
Thy ear, inur'd to charitable sounds
And pitying love, must feel the hateful wounds
Of jest obscene and vulgar ribaldry,
The ill-bred question, and the lew'd reply;

Brought by long habitude from bad to worse,
Must hear the frequent oath, the direful curse,
That latest weapon of the wretches' war,
And blasphemy, sad comrade of despair.
Now, Emma, now the last reflection make,
What thou wouldst follow, what thou must forsake:
By our ill-omen'd stars, and adverse Heaven,
No middle object to thy choice is given.
Or yield thy virtue to attain thy love;
Or leave a banish'd man, condemn'd in woods to rove.

EMMA.

O grief of heart! that our unhappy fates
Force thee to suffer what thy honour hates:
Mix thee amongst the bad; or make thee run
Too near the paths which virtue bids thee shun.
Yet with her Henry still let Emma go;
With him abhor the vice, but share the woe:
And sure my little heart can never err
Amidst the worst, if Henry still be there.
Our outward act is prompted from within;
And from the sinner's mind proceeds the sin:
By her own choice free virtue is approv'd;
Nor by the force of outward objects mov'd.
Who has assay'd no danger, gains no praise.
In a small isle, amidst the widest seas,
Triumphant Constancy has fix'd her seat,
In vain the Syrens sing, the tempests beat:
Their flattery she rejects, nor fears their threat.
For thee alone these little charms I drest:

Condemn'd them, or absolv'd them by thy test.
In comely figure rang'd my jewels shone,
Or negligently plac'd for thee alone:
For thee again they shall be laid aside;
The woman, Henry, shall put off her pride
For thee: my clothes, my sex, exchang'd for thee,
I'll mingle with the people's wretched lee;
O line extreme of human infamy!
Wanting the scissors, with these hands I'll tear
(If that obstructs my flight) this load of hair.
Black soot, or yellow walnut, shall disgrace
This little red and white of Emma's face.
These nails with scratches shall deform my breast,
Lest by my look or colour be express'd
The mark of aught high-born, or ever better dress'd.
Yet in this commerce, under this disguise,
Let me be grateful still to Henry's eyes;
Lost to the world, let me to him be known:
My fate I can absolve, if he shall own,
That, leaving all mankind, I love but him alone.

HENRY.

O wildest thoughts of an abandon'd mind!
Name, habit, parents, woman, left behind,
E'en honour dubious, thou preferr'st to go
Wild to the woods with me: said Emma so?
Or did I dream what Emma never said?
O guilty error! and O wretched maid!
Whose roving fancy would resolve the same
With him, who next shall tempt her easy fame;
And blow with empty words the susceptible flame.

Now why should doubtful terms thy mind perplex?
Confess thy frailty, and avow the sex:
No longer loose desire for constant love
Mistake; but say, 'tis man with whom thou long'st to rove.

EMMA.

Are there not poisons, racks, and flames, and swords,
That Emma thus must die by Henry's words?
Yet what could swords or poison, racks or flame,
But mangle and disjoint this brittle frame!
More fatal Henry's words; they murder Emma's fame.

And fall these sayings from that gentle tongue,
Where civil speech and soft persuasion hung;
Whose artful sweetness and harmonious strain,
Courting my grace, yet courting it in vain,
Call'd sighs, and tears, and wishes, to its aid;
And, whilst it Henry's glowing flame convey'd,
Still blame the coldness of the Nut-brown Maid?

Let envious jealousy and canker'd spite
Produce my actions to severest light,
And tax my open day, or secret night.
Did e'er my tongue speak my unguarded heart
The least inclin'd to play the wanton's part?
Did e'er my eye one inward thought reveal,
Which angels might not hear, and virgins tell?
And hast thou, Henry, in my conduct known
One fault, but that which I must never own,
That I, of all mankind, have lov'd but thee alone?

HENRY.

Vainly thou talk'st of loving me alone:
Each man is man; and all our sex is one.
False are our words, and fickle is our mind:
Nor in love's ritual can we ever find
Vows made to last, or promises to bind.

By nature prompted, and for empire made,
Alike by strength or cunning we invade:
When arm'd with rage we march against the foe,
We lift the battle-axe, and draw the bow:
When, fir'd with passion, we attack the fair,
Delusive sighs and brittle vows we bear;
Our falsehood and our arms have equal use;
As they our conquest or delight produce.
The foolish heart thou gav'st, again receive,
The only boon departing love can give.
To be less wretched, be no longer true;
What strives to fly thee, why shouldst thou pursue?
Forget the present flame, indulge a new;
Single the loveliest of the amorous youth;
Ask for his vow; but hope not for his truth.
The next man (and the next thou shalt believe)
Will pawn his gods, intending to deceive;
Will kneel, implore, persist, o'ercome, and leave.
Hence let thy Cupid aim his arrows right;
Be wise and false, shun trouble, seek delight;
Change thou the first, nor wait thy lover's flight.

Why shouldst thou weep? let nature judge our case;
I saw thee young and fair; pursued the chase

Of youth and beauty : I another saw
Fairer and younger : yielding to the law
Of our all-ruling mother, I pursued
More youth, more beauty : blest vicissitude!
My active heart still keeps its pristine flame ;
The object alter'd, the desire the same.
  This younger, fairer, pleads her rightful charms ;
With present power compels me to her arms.
And much I fear, from my subjected mind
(If beauty's force to constant love can bind),
That years may roll, ere in her turn the maid
Shall weep the fury of my love decay'd ;
And weeping follow me, as thou dost now,
With idle clamours of a broken vow.
  Nor can the wildness of thy wishes err
So wide, to hope that thou mayst live with her.
Love, well thou know'st, no partnership allows :
Cupid averse rejects divided vows :
Then from thy foolish heart, vain maid, remove
An useless sorrow, and an ill-starr'd love ;
And leave me, with the fair, at large in woods to rove.

EMMA.

  Are we in life through one great error led?
Is each man perjur'd, and each nymph betray'd?
Of the superior sex art thou the worst?
Am I of mine the most completely curst?
Yet let me go with thee ; and going prove,
From what I will endure, how much I love.
  This potent beauty, this triumphant fair,

This happy object of our different care,
Her let me follow; her let me attend
A servant (she may scorn the name of friend).
What she demands, incessant I'll prepare:
I'll weave her garlands; and I'll plait her hair:
My busy diligence shall deck her board
(For there at least I may approach my lord),
And, when her Henry's softer hours advise
His servant's absence, with dejected eyes
Far I'll recede, and sighs forbid to rise.
Yet, when increasing grief brings slow disease;
And ebbing life, on terms severe as these,
Will have its little lamp no longer fed;
When Henry's mistress shews him Emma dead;
Rescue my poor remains from vile neglect:
With virgin honours let my hearse be deckt,
And decent emblem; and at least persuade
This happy nymph, that Emma may be laid
Where thou, dear author of my death, where she,
With frequent eye my sepulchre may see.
The nymph amidst her joys may haply breathe
One pious sigh, reflecting on my death,
And the sad fate which she may one day prove,
Who hopes from Henry's vows eternal love.
And thou forsworn, thou cruel, as thou art,
If Emma's image ever touch'd thy heart;
Thou sure must give one thought, and drop one tear
To her, whom love abandon'd to despair;
To her, who, dying, on the wounded stone

Bid it in lasting characters be known,
That, of mankind, she lov'd but thee alone.

HENRY.

Hear, solemn Jove; and conscious Venus, hear;
And thou, bright maid, believe me whilst I swear;
No time, no change, no future flame, shall move
The well-plac'd basis of my lasting love.
O powerful virtue! O victorious fair!
At least excuse a trial too severe:
Receive the triumph, and forget the war.
No banish'd man, condemn'd in woods to rove,
Intreats thy pardon, and implores thy love:
No perjur'd knight desires to quit thy arms,
Fairest collection of thy sex's charms,
Crown of my love, and honour of my youth!
Henry, thy Henry, with eternal truth,
As thou mayst wish, shall all his life employ,
And found his glory in his Emma's joy.
In me behold the potent Edgar's heir,
Illustrious earl: him terrible in war
Let Loyre confess, for she has felt his sword,
And trembling fled before the British lord.
Him great in peace and wealth fair Deva knows;
For she amidst his spacious meadows flows;
Inclines her urn upon his fatten'd lands,
And sees his numerous herds imprint her sands.
And thou, my fair, my dove, shalt raise thy thought
To greatness next to empire; shalt be brought
With solemn pomp to my paternal seat:

Where peace and plenty on thy word shall wait.
Music and song shall wake the marriage-day:
And, whilst the priests accuse the bride's delay,
Myrtles and roses shall obstruct her way.
  Friendship shall still thy evening feasts adorn;
And blooming peace shall ever bless thy morn.
Succeeding years their happy race shall run,
And age unheeded by delight come on;
While yet superior love shall mock his power:
And when old Time shall turn the fated hour,
Which only can our well-tied knot unfold;
What rests of both, one sepulchre shall hold.
  Hence then for ever from my Emma's breast
(That heaven of softness, and that seat of rest)
Ye doubts and fears, and all that know to move
Tormenting grief, and all that trouble love,
Scatter'd by winds recede, and wild in forests rove.

EMMA.

  O day the fairest sure that ever rose!
Period and end of anxious Emma's woes!
Sire of her joy, and source of her delight;
O! wing'd with pleasure take thy happy flight,
And give each future morn a tincture of thy white.
Yet tell thy votary, potent queen of love,
Henry, my Henry, will he never rove?
Will he be ever kind, and just, and good?
And is there yet no mistress in the wood?
None, none there is; the thought was rash and vain;
A false idea, and a fancied pain.

Doubt shall for ever quit my strengthen'd heart,
And anxious jealousy's corroding smart;
Nor other inmate shall inhabit there,
But soft Belief, young Joy, and pleasing Care:
  Hence let the tides of plenty ebb and flow,
And fortune's various gale unheeded blow.
If at my feet the suppliant goddess stands,
And sheds her treasure with unwearied hands;
Her present favour cautious I'll embrace,
And not unthankful use the proffer'd grace:
If she reclaims the temporary boon,
And tries her pinions, fluttering to be gone;
Secure of mind, I'll obviate her intent,
And unconcern'd return the goods she lent.
Nor happiness can I, nor misery feel,
From any turn of her fantastic wheel:
Friendship's great laws, and love's superior powers,
Must mark the colour of my future hours.
From the events which thy commands create
I must my blessings or my sorrows date;
And Henry's will must dictate Emma's fate.
  Yet while with close delight and inward pride
(Which from the world my careful soul shall hide)
I see thee, lord and end of my desire,
Exalted high as virtue can require;
With power invested, and with pleasure cheer'd;
Sought by the good, by the oppressor fear'd;
Loaded and blest with all the affluent store,
Which human vows at smoking shrines implore;
Grateful and humble grant me to employ

My life subservient only to thy joy ;
And at my death to bless thy kindness shown
To her, who of mankind could love but thee alone.

While thus the constant pair alternate said,
Joyful above them and around them play'd
Angels and sportive loves, a numerous crowd ;
Smiling they clapp'd their wings, and low they
bow'd :
They tumbled all their little quivers o'er,
To choose propitious shafts, a precious store ;
That, when their god should take his future darts,
To strike (however rarely) constant hearts,
His happy skill might proper arms employ,
All tipp'd with pleasure, and all wing'd with joy :
And those, they vow'd, whose lives should imitate
These lovers' constancy, should share their fate.
The queen of beauty stopp'd her bridled doves ;
Approv'd the little labour of the loves ;
Was proud and pleas'd the mutual vow to hear ;
And to the triumph call'd the god of war :
Soon as she calls, the god is always near.
Now, Mars, she said, let Fame exalt her voice :
Nor let thy conquests only be her choice :
But, when she sings great Edward from the field
Return'd, the hostile spear and captive shield
In Concord's temple hung, and Gallia taught to
yield :
And when, as prudent Saturn shall complete
The years design'd to perfect Britain's state,

The swift-wing'd power shall take her trump again,
To sing her favourite Anna's wondrous reign;
To recollect unwearied Marlborough's toils,
Old Rufus' hall unequal to his spoils;
The British soldier from his high command
Glorious, and Gaul thrice vanquish'd by his hand:
Let her at least perform what I desire;
With second breath the vocal brass inspire;
And tell the nations, in no vulgar strain,
What wars I manage, and what wreaths I gain.
And, when thy tumults and thy fights are past;
And when thy laurels at my feet are cast;
Faithful mayst thou, like British Henry, prove:
And, Emma-like, let me return thy love.
  Renown'd for truth, let all thy sons appear;
And constant beauty shall reward their care.
  Mars smil'd, and bow'd: the Cyprian deity
Turn'd to the glorious ruler of the sky;
And thou, she smiling said, great god of days
And verse, behold my deed, and sing my praise,
As on the British earth, my favourite isle,
Thy gentle rays and kindest influence smile,
Through all her laughing fields and verdant groves,
Proclaim with joy these memorable loves.
From every annual course let one great day
To celebrated sports and floral play
Be set aside; and, in the softest lays
Of thy poetic sons, be solemn praise
And everlasting marks of honour paid,
To the true lover, and the Nut-brown Maid.

AN ODE,

HUMBLY INSCRIBED TO THE QUEEN, ON THE GLORIOUS SUCCESS OF HER MAJESTY'S ARMS. MDCCVI.

WRITTEN IN IMITATION OF SPENSER'S STYLE.

" Te non paventis funera Galliæ,
Duræque tellus audit Iberiæ:
Te cæde gaudentes Sicambri
Compositis venerantur armis." Hor.

PREFACE.

When I first thought of writing upon this occasion, I found the ideas so great and numerous, that I judged them more proper for the warmth of an Ode, than for any other sort of poetry: I therefore set Horace before me for a pattern, and particularly his famous ode, the fourth of the fourth book,

" Qualem ministrum fulminis alitem," &c.

which he wrote in praise of Drusus after his expedition into Germany, and of Augustus upon his happy choice of that general. And in the following poem, though I have endeavoured to imitate all the great strokes of that ode, I have taken the liberty to go off from it, and to add variously, as the subject and my own imagination carried me. As to the style, the choice I made of following the ode in Latin determined me in English to the stanza; and herein it was impossible not to have a mind to follow our great countryman Spenser; which I have done (as well at least as I could) in the manner of my expression, and the turn of my number: having only added one verse to his stanza, which I thought made the number more harmonious; and avoided such of his words as I found too obsolete. I have, however, retained some few of them, to make the colouring look more like Spenser's. *Behest*, command; *band*, army; *prowess*, strength; I *weet*, I know; I *ween*, I think; *whilom*, heretofore; and two or three more of that kind, which I hope the ladies will pardon me, and not judge my Muse less handsome, though for once she appears in a farthingale. I have also, in Spenser's manner, used *Cæsar* for the emperor, *Boya* for Bavaria, *Bavar* for that prince, *Ister* for Danube, *Iberia* for Spain, &c.

That noble part of the Ode which I just now mentioned,

> " Gens, quæ, cremato fortis ab Ilio
> Jactata Tuscis æquoribus," &c.

where Horace praises the Romans as being descended from Æneas, I have turned to the honour of the British nation, descended from Brute, likewise a Trojan. That this Brute, fourth or fifth from Æneas, settled in England, and built London, which is called Troja Nova, or Troynovante, is a story which (I think) owes its original, if not to Geoffry of Monmouth, at least to the Monkish writers; yet it is not rejected by our great Camden; and is told by Milton, as if (at least) he was pleased with it, though possibly he does not believe it: however, it carries a poetical authority, which is sufficient for our purpose. It is as certain that Brute came into England, as that Æneas went into Italy; and upon the supposition of these facts, Virgil wrote the best poem that the world ever read, and Spenser paid Queen Elizabeth the greatest compliment.

I need not obviate one piece of criticism, that I bring my hero

"From burning Troy, and Xanthus red with blood:"

whereas he was not born when that city was destroyed. Virgil, in the case of his own Æneas relating to Dido, will stand as a sufficient proof, that a man in his poetical capacity is not accountable for a little fault in chronology.

My two great examples, Horace and Spenser, in many things resemble each other: both have a height of imagination, and a majesty of expression in describing the sublime; and both know to temper those talents, and sweeten the description, so as to make it lovely as well as pompous: both have equally that agreeable manner of mixing morality with their story, and that Curiosa Felicitas in the choice of their diction, which every writer aims at, and so very few have reached: both are particularly fine in their images, and knowing in their numbers. Leaving therefore our two masters to the consideration and study of those who design to excel in poetry, I only beg leave to add, that it is long since I have (or at least ought to have) quitted Parnassus, and all the flowery roads on that side the country; though I thought myself indispensably obliged, upon the present occasion, to take a little journey in those parts.

AN ODE.

When great Augustus govern'd ancient Rome,
And sent his conquering bands to foreign wars;
Abroad when dreaded, and belov'd at home,
He saw his fame increasing with his years;
Horace, great bard! (so Fate ordain'd) arose,
And, bold as were his countrymen in fight,
Snatch'd their fair actions from degrading prose,
And set their battles in eternal light:
High as their trumpets tune his lyre he strung,
And with his prince's arms he moraliz'd his song.

When bright Eliza rul'd Britannia's state,
Widely distributing her high commands,
And boldly wise, and fortunately great,
Freed the glad nations from tyrannic bands;
An equal genius was in Spenser found;
To the high theme he match'd his noble lays;
He travell'd England o'er on fairy ground,
In mystic notes to sing his monarch's praise:
Reciting wondrous truths in pleasing dreams,
He deck'd Eliza's head with Gloriana's beams.

But, greatest Anna! while thy arms pursue
Paths of renown, and climb ascents of fame,
Which nor Augustus, nor Eliza knew;
What poet shall be found to sing thy name?
What numbers shall record, what tongue shall say
Thy wars on land, thy triumphs on the main?
O fairest model of imperial sway!
What equal pen shall write thy wondrous reign?
Who shall attempts and feats of arms rehearse,
Not yet by story told, nor parallel'd by verse?

Me all too mean for such a task I weet:
Yet, if the Sovereign Lady deigns to smile,
I'll follow Horace with impetuous heat,
And clothe the verse in Spenser's native style.
By these examples rightly taught to sing,
And smit with pleasure of my country's praise,
Stretching the plumes of an uncommon wing,
High as Olympus I my flight will raise;

And latest times shall in my numbers read
Anna's immortal fame, and Marlborough's hardy
deed.

As the strong eagle in the silent wood,
Mindless of warlike rage and hostile care,
Plays round the rocky cliff or crystal flood,
Till by Jove's high behests call'd out to war,
And charg'd with thunder of his angry king,
His bosom with the vengeful message glows;
Upward the noble bird directs his wing,
And, towering round his master's earth-born foes,
Swift he collects his fatal stock of ire,
Lifts his fierce talon high, and darts the forked fire:

Sedate and calm thus victor Marlborough sate,
Shaded with laurels, in his native land,
Till Anna calls him from his soft retreat,
And gives her second thunder to his hand.
Then, leaving sweet repose and gentle ease,
With ardent speed he seeks the distant foe;
Marching o'er hills and vales, o'er rocks and seas,
He meditates, and strikes the wondrous blow.
Our thought flies slower than our general's fame:
Grasps he the bolt? we ask—when he has hurl'd
the flame.

When fierce Bavar on Judoign's spacious plain
Did from afar the British chief behold,
Betwixt despair, and rage, and hope, and pain,

Something within his warring bosom roll'd :
He views that favourite of indulgent fame,
Whom whilom he had met on Ister's shore ;
Too well, alas ! the man he knows the same,
Whose prowess there repell'd the Boyan power,
And sent them trembling through the frighted lands,
Swift as the whirlwind drives Arabia's scatter'd
sands.

His former losses he forgets to grieve ;
Absolves his fate, if with a kinder ray
It now would shine, and only give him leave
To balance the account of Blenheim's day.
So the fell lion in the lonely glade,
His side still smarting with the hunter's spear,
Though deeply wounded, no way yet dismay'd,
Roars terrible, and meditates new war ;
In sullen fury traverses the plain,
To find the venturous foe, and battle him again.

Misguided prince, no longer urge thy fate,
Nor tempt the hero to unequal war ;
Fam'd in misfortune, and in ruin great,
Confess the force of Marlborough's stronger star.
Those laurel groves (the merits of thy youth),
Which thou from [1] Mahomet didst greatly gain,

[1] The Elector of Bavaria had formerly acquired great reputation by the success of his arms against the Turks, particularly in obliging them to raise the siege of Vienna, after it had continued 59 days, in September 1683, with the loss of seventy-five thousand men and their baggage.

While, bold assertor of resistless truth,
Thy sword did godlike liberty maintain,
Must from thy brow their falling honours shed,
And their transplanted wreaths must deck a worthier head.

Yet cease the ways of Providence to blame,
And human faults with human grief confess,
'Tis thou art chang'd, while Heaven is still the same;
From thy ill councils date the ill success.
Impartial Justice holds her equal scales,
Till stronger virtue does the weight incline;
If over thee thy glorious foe prevails,
He now defends the cause that once was thine.
Righteous the war, the champion shall subdue;
For Jove's great handmaid, Power, must Jove's decrees pursue.

Hark! the dire trumpets sound their shrill alarms!
Auverquerque,[1] branch'd from the renown'd Nassaus,
Hoary in war, and bent beneath his arms,
His glorious sword with dauntless courage draws.
When anxious Britain mourn'd her parting lord,
And all of William that was mortal died;
The faithful hero had receiv'd his sword

[1] Monsieur Auverquerque who, in the year 1704, and the succeeding campaigns, was appointed to the command of the Dutch forces. He was in great favour with King William, and present at his death.

From his expiring master's much-lov'd side.
Oft from its fatal ire has Louis flown,
Where'er great William led, or Maese and Sambre
run.

But brandish'd high, in an ill-omen'd hour
To thee, proud Gaul, behold thy justest fear,
The master sword, disposer of thy power:
'Tis that which Cæsar gave the British peer.
He took the gift: nor ever will I sheathe
This steel (so Anna's high behests ordain),
The general said, unless by glorious death
Absolv'd, till conquest has confirm'd your reign.
Returns like these our mistress bids us make,
When from a foreign prince a gift her Britons take.

And now fierce Gallia rushes on her foes,
Her force augmented by the Boyan bands;
So Volga's stream, increas'd by mountain snows,
Rolls with new fury down through Russia's lands.
Like two great rocks against the raging tide
(If Virtue's force with Nature's we compare),
Unmov'd the two united chiefs abide,
Sustain the impulse, and receive the war.
Round their firm sides in vain the tempest beats;
And still the foaming wave with lessen'd power
retreats.

The rage dispers'd, the glorious pair advance,
With mingled anger and collected might,

To turn the war, and tell aggressing France,
How Britain's sons and Britain's friends can fight.
On conquest fix'd, and covetous of fame,
Behold them rushing through the Gallic host:
Through standing corn so runs the sudden flame,
Or eastern winds along Sicilia's coast.
They deal their terrors to the adverse nation:
Pale death attends their arms, and ghastly deso-
lation.

But whilst with fiercest ire Bellona glows,
And Europe rather hopes than fears her fate;
While Britain presses her afflicted foes;
What horror damps the strong, and quells the great!
Whence look the soldier's cheeks dismay'd and pale?
Erst ever dreadful, know they now to dread?
The hostile troops, I ween, almost prevail;
And the pursuers only not recede.
Alas! their lessen'd rage proclaims their grief!
For, anxious, lo! they crowd around their falling
chief.

I thank thee, Fate, exclaims the fierce Bavar:
Let Boya's trumpet grateful Iös sound:
I saw him fall, their thunderbolt of war:—
Ever to vengeance sacred be the ground.—
Vain wish! short joy! the hero mounts again
In greater glory, and with fuller light:
The evening-star so falls into the main,
To rise at morn more prevalently bright.

He rises safe,[1] but near, too near his side,
A good man's grievous loss, a faithful servant died.

Propitious Mars! the battle is regain'd:
The foe with lessen'd wrath disputes the field:
The Briton fights, by favouring gods sustain'd:
Freedom must live; and lawless power must yield.
Vain now the tales which fabling poets tell,
That wavering Conquest still desires to rove!
In Marlborough's camp the goddess knows to dwell:
Long as the hero's life remains her love.
Again France flies, again the duke pursues,
And on Ramilia's plains he Blenheim's fame renews.

Great thanks, O captain great in arms! receive
From thy triumphant country's public voice;
Thy country greater thanks can only give
To Anne, to her who made those arms her choice.
Recording Schellenberg's[2] and Blenheim's toils,
We dreaded lest thou shouldst those toils repeat:
We view'd the palace charg'd with Gallic spoils,
And in those spoils we thought thy praise complete.
For never Greek we deem'd, nor Roman knight,
In characters like these did e'er his acts indite.

1 At the Battle of Ramilies the Duke of Marlborough was twice in the most imminent danger; once by a fall from his horse, and a second time by a cannon shot that took off the head of Colonel Bringfield as he was holding the stirrup for his Grace to remount.

2 Where the Duke of Marlborough gained a complete victory over 16,000 Bavarians in July, 1704.

Yet, mindless still of ease, thy virtue flies
A pitch to old and modern times unknown:
Those goodly deeds which we so highly prize
Imperfect seem, great chief, to thee alone.
Those heights, where William's virtue might have staid,
And on the subject world look'd safely down,
By Marlborough pass'd, the props and steps were made,
Sublimer yet to raise his queen's renown:
Still gaining more, still slighting what he gain'd,
Nought done the hero deem'd, while aught undone remain'd.

When swift-wing'd rumour told the mighty Gaul,
How lessen'd from the field Bavar was fled;
He wept the swiftness of the champion's fall;
And thus the royal treaty-breaker said:
And lives he yet, the great, the lost Bavar,
Ruin to Gallia in the name of friend?
Tell me, how far has Fortune been severe?
Has the foe's glory, or our grief, an end?
Remains there of the fifty thousand lost,
To save our threaten'd realm, or guard our shatter'd coast?

To the close rock the frighten'd raven flies,
Soon as the rising eagle cuts the air:
The shaggy wolf unseen and trembling lies,
When the hoarse roar proclaims the lion near.

Ill-starr'd did we our forts and lines forsake,
To dare our British foes to open fight:
Our conquest we by stratagem should make:
Our triumph had been founded in our flight.
'Tis ours, by craft and by surprise to gain:
'Tis theirs, to meet in arms, and battle in the plain.

The ancient father of this hostile brood,
Their boasted Brute, undaunted snatch'd his gods
From burning Troy, and Xanthus red with blood,
And fix'd on silver Thames his dire abodes:
And this be Troynovante, he said, the seat
By Heaven ordain'd, my sons, your lasting place:
Superior here to all the bolts of fate
Live, mindful of the author of your race,
Whom neither Greece, nor war, nor want, nor flame,
Nor great Peleides' arm, nor Juno's rage could tame.

Their Tudor's hence, and Stuart's offspring flow:
Hence Edward, dreadful with his sable shield,
Talbot to Gallia's power eternal foe,
And Seymour, fam'd in council or in field:
Hence Nevil, great to settle or dethrone,
And Drake and Ca'ndish, terrors of the sea:
Hence Butler's sons, o'er land and ocean known,
Herbert's and Churchill's warring progeny:
Hence the long roll which Gallia should conceal:
For, oh! who vanquish'd, loves the victor's fame to tell?

Envied Britannia, sturdy as the oak,
Which on her mountain-top she proudly bears,
Eludes the axe, and sprouts against the stroke;
Strong from her wounds, and greater by her wars.
And as those teeth, which Cadmus sow'd in earth,
Produc'd new youth, and furnish'd fresh supplies:
So with young vigour, and succeeding birth,
Her losses more than recompens'd arise;
And ev'ry age she with a race is crown'd,
For letters more polite, in battles more renown'd.

Obstinate power, whom nothing can repel;
Not the fierce Saxon, nor the cruel Dane,
Nor deep impression of the Norman steel,
Nor Europe's force amass'd by envious Spain,
Nor France on universal sway intent,
Oft breaking leagues, and oft renewing wars;
Nor (frequent bane of weaken'd government)
Their own intestine feuds and mutual jars:
Those feuds and jars, in which I trusted more,
Than in my troops, and fleets, and all the Gallic power.

To fruitful Rheims, or fair Lutetia's gate,
What tidings shall the messenger convey?
Shall the loud herald our success relate,
Or mitred priest appoint the solemn day?
Alas! my praises they no more must sing;
They to my statue now must bow no more:
Broken, repuls'd is their immortal king:

Fallen, fallen for ever, is the Gallic power.—
The woman chief is master of the war:
Earth, she has freed by arms, and vanquish'd
Heaven by prayer.

While thus the ruin'd foe's despair commends
Thy council and thy deed, victorious queen,
What shall thy subjects say, and what thy friends?
How shall thy triumphs in our joy be seen?
Oh! deign to let the eldest of the nine
Recite Britannia great, and Gallia free:
Oh! with her sister sculpture let her join
To raise, great Anne, the monument to thee;
To thee, of all our good the sacred spring;
To thee, our dearest dread; to thee, our softer king.

Let Europe sav'd the column high erect,
Than Trajan's higher, or than Antonine's;
Where sembling art may carve the fair effect
And full achievement of the great designs.
In a calm Heaven, and a serener air,
Sublime the queen shall on the summit stand,
From danger far, as far remov'd from fear,
And pointing down to earth her dread command.
All winds, all storms, that threaten human woe,
Shall sink beneath her feet, and spread their rage
below.

Their fleets shall strive, by winds and waters
toss'd,

Till the young Austrian on Iberia's strand,
Great as Æneas on the Latian coast,
Shall fix his foot: and this, be this the land,
Great Jove, where I for ever will remain,
(The empire's other hope shall say) and here
Vanquish'd, intomb'd I'll lie; or, crown'd, I'll reign!
O virtue, to thy British mother dear!
Like the fam'd Trojan suffer and abide;
For Anne is thine, I ween, as Venus was his guide.

There, in eternal characters engrav'd,
Vigo,[1] and Gibraltar, and Barcelone,
Their force destroy'd, their privileges sav'd,
Shall Anna's terrors and her mercies own:
Spain, from th' usurper Bourbon's arms retriev'd,
Shall with new life and grateful joy appear,
Numbering the wonders which that youth achiev'd,
Whom Anna clad in arms and sent to war;
Whom Anna sent to claim Iberia's throne;
And made him more than king, in calling him her son.

There Isther, pleas'd by Blenheim's glorious field,
Rolling shall bid his eastern waves declare
Germania sav'd by Britain's ample shield,

[1] Vigo was surprised by the Duke of Ormond and Sir George Rooke, and the galleons taken and destroyed in the year 1702; Gibraltar by Sir George Rooke in 1704; and Barcelona by the Prince of Hesse and the Earl of Peterborough in 1705.

And bleeding Gaul afflicted by her spear;
Shall bid them mention Marlborough on that shore,
Leading his islanders, renown'd in arms,
Through climes, where never British chief before
Or pitch'd his camp, or sounded his alarms;
Shall bid them bless the queen, who made his streams
Glorious as those of Boyne, and safe as those of Thames.

Brabantia, clad with fields, and crown'd with towers,
With decent joy shall her deliverer meet;
Shall own thy arms, great queen, and bless thy powers,
Laying the keys beneath thy subject's feet.
Flandria, by plenty made the home of war,
Shall weep her crime, and bow to Charles restor'd;
With double vows shall bless thy happy care,
In having drawn, and having sheath'd the sword;
From these their sister provinces shall know
How Anne supports a friend, and how forgives a foe.

Bright swords, and crested helms, and pointed spears,
In artful piles around the work shall lie;
And shields indented deep in ancient wars,
Blazon'd with signs of Gallic heraldry;
And standards with distinguish'd honours bright,
Marks of high power and national command,

Which Valois' sons, and Bourbon's bore in fight,
Or gave to Foix' or Montmorency's hand:
Great spoils, which Gallia must to Britain yield,
From Cressy's battle sav'd, to grace Ramilia's field.

And, as fine art the spaces may dispose,
The knowing thought and curious eye shall see
Thy emblem, gracious queen, the British rose,
Type of sweet rule and gentle majesty:
The northern thistle, whom no hostile hand
Unhurt too rudely may provoke, I ween;
Hibernia's harp, device of her command,
And parent of her mirth, shall there be seen:
Thy vanquish'd lilies, France, decay'd and torn,
Shall with disorder'd pomp the lasting work adorn.

Beneath, great queen, oh! very far beneath,
Near to the ground, and on the humble base,
To save herself from darkness and from death,
That Muse desires the last, the lowest place;
Who, though unmeet, yet touch'd the trembling string,
For the fair fame of Anne and Albion's land,
Who durst of war and martial fury sing;
And when thy will, and when thy subject's hand,
Had quell'd those wars, and bid that fury cease,
Hangs up her grateful harp to conquest and to peace.

HER RIGHT NAME.

As Nancy at her toilet sat,
Admiring this, and blaming that;
Tell me, she said; but tell me true;
The nymph who could your heart subdue.
What sort of charms does she possess?
Absolve me, fair one: I'll confess
With pleasure, I replied. Her hair,
In ringlets rather dark than fair,
Does down her ivory bosom roll,
And, hiding half, adorns the whole.
In her high forehead's fair half round
Love sits in open triumph crown'd:
He in the dimple of her chin,
In private state by friends is seen.
Her eyes are neither black nor gray;
Nor fierce nor feeble is their ray;
Their dubious lustre seems to show
Something that speaks nor yes, nor no.
Her lips no living bard, I weet,
May say, how red, how round, how sweet;
Old Homer only could indite
Their vagrant grace and soft delight:
They stand recorded in his book,
When Helen smil'd, and Hebe spoke—

The gipsy, turning to her glass,
Too plainly show'd she knew the face;
And which am I most like, she said,
Your Cloe, or your Nut-brown Maid?

CANTATA.

SET BY MONSIEUR GALLIARD.

RECIT.

Beneath a verdant laurel's ample shade,
His lyre to mournful numbers strung,
Horace, immortal bard, supinely laid,
To Venus thus address'd the song:
Ten thousand little loves around,
Listening, dwelt on every sound.

ARIET.

Potent Venus, bid thy son
Sound no more his dire alarms.
Youth on silent wings is flown:
Graver years come rolling on.
Spare my age, unfit for arms:
Safe and humble let me rest,
From all amorous care releas'd.
Potent Venus, bid thy son
Sound no more his dire alarms.

RECIT.

Yet, Venus, why do I each morn prepare
The fragrant wreath for Cloe's hair?
Why do I all day lament and sigh,
Unless the beauteous maid be nigh?
And why all night pursue her in my dreams,
Through flowery meads and crystal streams?

RECIT.

Thus sung the bard; and thus the goddess spoke:
Submissive bow to Love's imperious yoke:
Every state, and every age
Shall own my rule, and fear my rage:
Compell'd by me, thy Muse shall prove,
That all the world was born to love.

ARIET.

Bid thy destin'd lyre discover
Soft desire and gentle pain:
Often praise, and always love her:
Through her ear, her heart obtain.
Verse shall please, and sighs shall move her,
Cupid does with Phœbus reign.

LINES WRITTEN IN AN OVID.[1]

Ovid is the surest guide
  You can name to show the way
To any woman, maid, or bride,
  Who resolves to go astray.

A TRUE MAID.

No, no; for my virginity,
  When I lose that, says Rose, I'll die:
Behind the elms, last night, cried Dick,
  Rose, were you not extremely sick?

[1] Translated from the following Madrigal of Gilbert, sur l'Art d'Aimer d'Ovide.

A PHILIS.

Cette lecture est sans égale,
Ce livre est un petit dédale,
Ou l'esprit prend plaisir d'errer,
Philis, suivez les pas d'Ovide,
C'est le plus agréable guide,
Qu'on peut choisir pour s'égarer.

ANOTHER.

Ten months after Florimel happen'd to wed,
And was brought in a laudable manner to bed,
She warbled her groans with so charming a voice,
That one half of the parish was stunn'd with the
noise ;
But when Florimel deign'd to lie privately in,
Ten months before she and her spouse were a-kin,
She chose with such prudence her pangs to conceal,
That her nurse, nay, her midwife, scarce heard her
once squeal.
Learn, husbands, from hence, for the peace of your
lives,
That maids make not half such a tumult as wives.

A REASONABLE AFFLICTION.

On his death-bead poor Lubin lies ;
His spouse is in despair :
With frequent sobs, and mutual cries,
They both express their care.

A different cause, says parson Sly,
The same effect may give :
Poor Lubin fears that he shall die ;
His wife, that he may live.

ANOTHER.

From her own native France as old Alison past,
She approach'd English Nell with neglect or with malice,
That the slattern had left, in the hurry and haste,
Her lady's complexion and eye-brows at Calais.

ANOTHER.

Her eye-brow box one morning lost,
(The best of folks are oftenest crost)
Sad Helen thus to Jenny said,
Her careless but afflicted maid,
Put me to bed then, wretched Jane;
Alas! when shall I rise again?
I can behold no mortal now:
For what's an eye without a brow.

ON THE SAME SUBJECT.

In a dark corner of the house
Poor Helen sits, and sobs and cries;
She will not see her loving spouse,
Nor her more dear picquet-allies:
Unless she find her eye-brows,
She'll e'en weep out her eyes.

ON THE SAME SUBJECT.

HELEN was just slipt into bed:
Her eye-brows on the toilet lay:
Away the kitten with them fled,
As fees belonging to her prey.

For this misfortune careless Jane,
Assure yourself, was loudly rated:
And madam, getting up again,
With her own hand the mouse-trap baited.

On little things, as sages write,
Depends our human joy or sorrow:
If we don't catch a mouse to-night,
Alas! no eye-brows for to-morrow.

PHILLIS'S AGE.

How old may Phillis be, you ask,
Whose beauty thus all hearts engages?
To answer is no easy task:
For she has really two ages.

Stiff in brocade, and pinch'd in stays,
Her patches, paint, and jewels on;
All day let envy view her face,
And Phillis is but twenty-one.

Paint, patches, jewels laid aside,
  At night astronomers agree,
The evening has the day belied;
  And Phillis is some forty-three.

FORMA BONUM FRAGILE.

WHAT a frail thing is beauty! says baron Le Cras,
Perceiving his mistress had one eye of glass:
    And scarcely had he spoke it,
When she more confus'd as more angry she grew,
By a negligent rage prov'd the maxim too true:
    She dropt the eye, and broke it.

A CRITICAL MOMENT

HOW capricious were Nature and Art to poor Nell!
She was painting her cheeks at the time her nose
    fell.

AN EPIGRAM.

WRITTEN TO THE DUKE DE NOALLES.

VAIN the concern which you express,
That uncall'd Alard will possess
  Your house and coach, both day and night,
And that Macbeth was haunted less
  By Banquo's restless spright.

With fifteen thousand pounds a year,
Do you complain, you cannot bear
  An ill, you may so soon retrieve?
Good Alard, faith, is modester
  By much, than you believe.

Lend him but fifty louis-d'or;
And you shall never see him more:
  Take the advice; probatum est.
Why do the gods indulge our store,
  But to secure our rest?

EPILOGUE TO PHÆDRA AND HIPPOLITUS.[1]

BY MR. EDMUND SMITH. SPOKEN BY MRS. OLDFIELD, WHO ACTED ISMENA.

Ladies, to-night your pity I implore
For one, who never troubled you before;
An Oxford man, extremely read in Greek,
Who from Euripides makes Phædra speak;

[1] This excellent tragedy, although performed by Betterton, Booth, Mrs. Barry, and Mrs. Oldfield, met with but a very cold reception from the public on its first appearance. In the Spectator, No. 18, Mr. Addison says—"Would one think it was possible (at a time when an author lived that was able to write the Phædra and Hippolitus) for a people to be so stupidly fond of the Italian opera, as scarce to give a third day's hearing to that admirable tragedy." The prologue to it was written by Mr. Addison.

And comes to town to let us moderns know,
How women lov'd two thousand years ago.
  If that be all, said I, e'en burn your play:
Egad! we know all that, as well as they:
Show us the youthful, handsome charioteer,
Firm in his seat, and running his career;
Our souls would kindle with as generous flames,
As e'er inspir'd the ancient Grecian dames:
Every Ismena would resign her breast;
And every dear Hippolitus be blest.
  But, as it is, six flouncing Flanders mares
Are even as good as any two of theirs:
And if Hippolitus can but contrive
To buy the gilded chariot, John can drive.
  Now of the bustle you have seen to-day,
And Phædra's morals in this scholar's play,
Something at least in justice should be said;
But this Hippolitus so fills one's head——
Well! Phædra liv'd as chastely as she could!
For she was father Jove's own flesh and blood.
Her awkward love indeed was oddly fated;
She and her Poly were too near related;
And yet that scruple had been laid aside,
If honest Theseus had but fairly died:
But when he came, what needed he to know,
But that all matters stood in statu quo?
There was no harm, you see; or grant there were,
She might want conduct; but he wanted care.
'Twas in a husband little less than rude,
Upon his wife's retirement to intrude—

He should have sent a night or two before,
That he would come exact at such an hour;
Then he had turn'd all tragedy to jest;
Found every thing contribute to his rest;
The picquet-friend dismiss'd, the coast all clear,
And spouse alone impatient for her dear.
  But if these gay reflections come too late,
To keep the guilty Phædra from her fate;
If your more serious judgment must condemn
The dire effects of her unhappy flame:
Yet, ye chaste matrons, and ye tender fair,
Let love and innocence engage your care:
My spotless flames to your protection take;
And spare poor Phædra for Ismena's sake.

EPILOGUE TO LUCIUS.[1]

A TRAGEDY, BY MRS. DE LA RIVIERE MANLEY.

SPOKEN BY MRS. HORTON.

The female author who recites to-day,
Trusts to her sex the merit of her play.
Like father Bayes securely she sits down:
Pit, box, and gallery, 'gad! all's our own.

[1] This play was acted at Drury-lane, in 1717, with success. In the dedication to Sir Richard Steele, who wrote a prologue to it, the author apologizes for the severity of her former writings against him.

In ancient Greece, she says, when Sappho writ,
By their applause the critics show'd their wit,
They tun'd their voices to her lyric string;
Though they could all do something more than sing.
But one exception to this fact we find;
That booby Phaon only was unkind,
An ill-bred boat-man, rough as waves and wind.
From Sappho down through all succeeding ages,
And now on French, or on Italian stages,
Rough satires, sly remarks, ill-natur'd speeches,
Are always aim'd at poets that wear breeches.
Arm'd with Longinus, or with Rapin, no man
Drew a sharp pen upon a naked woman.
The blustering bully, in our neighbouring streets,
Scorns to attack the female that he meets:
Fearless the petticoat contemns his frowns:
The hoop secures whatever it surrounds.
The many-colour'd gentry there above,
By turns are rul'd by tumult, and by love:
And while their sweethearts their attention fix,
Suspend the din of their damn'd clattering sticks.
Now, Sirs——
To you our author makes her soft request,
Who speak the kindest, and who write the best,
Your sympathetic hearts she hopes to move,
From tender friendship, and endearing love.
If Petrarch's Muse did Laura's wit rehearse;
And Cowley flatter'd dear Orinda's verse;
She hopes from you—Pox take her hopes and fears:
I plead her sex's claim; what matters hers?

By our full power of beauty we think fit
To damn the salique law impos'd on wit:
We'll try the empire you so long have boasted;
And if we are not prais'd, we'll not be toasted.
Approve what one of us presents to-night;
Or every mortal woman here shall write:
Rural, pathetic, narrative, sublime,
We'll write to you, and make you write in rhyme;
Female remarks shall take up all your time.
Your time, poor souls! we'll take your very money;
Female third days shall come so quick upon ye.
As long as we have eyes, or hands, or breath,
We'll look, or write, or talk you all to death.
Unless you yield for better and for worse:
Then the she-pegasus shall gain the course;
And the gray mare will prove the better horse.

THE THIEF AND THE CORDELIER,

A BALLAD. TO THE TUNE OF KING JOHN AND THE ABBOT OF CANTERBURY.

WHO has e'er been at Paris must needs know the
Greve,
The fatal retreat of the unfortunate brave:
Where honour and justice most oddly contribute,
To ease heroes' pains by a halter and gibbet,
Derry down, down, hey derry down.

There death breaks the shackles which force had put on;
And the hangman completes what the judge but begun;
There the squire of the pad, and the knight of the post,
Find their pains no more balk'd, and their hopes no more cross'd.
Derry down, &c.

Great claims are there made, and great secrets are known;
And the king, and the law, and the thief has his own;
But my hearers cry out, What a deuce dost thou ail?
Cut off thy reflections, and give us thy tale.
Derry down, &c.

'Twas there then, in civil respect to harsh laws,
And for want of false witness, to back a bad cause,
A Norman, though late, was obliged to appear;
And who to assist, but a grave Cordelier?
Derry down, &c.

The squire, whose good grace was to open the scene,
Seem'd not in great haste, that the show should begin:
Now fitted the halter, now travers'd the cart;
And often took leave; but was loth to depart.
Derry down, &c.

What frightens you thus, my good son? say the priest:

You murder'd, are sorry, and have been confess'd.
O father! my sorrow will scarce save my bacon:
For 'twas not that I murder'd, but that I was taken.
Derry down, &c.

Pugh! prithee ne'er trouble thy head with such fancies:
Rely on the aid you shall have from Saint Francis;
If the money you promis'd be brought to the chest,
You have only to die: let the church do the rest.
Derry down, &c.

And what will folks say, if they see you afraid?
It reflects upon me, as I knew not my trade:
Courage, friend; to-day is your period of sorrow;
And things will go better, believe me, to-morrow.
Derry down, &c.

To-morrow? our hero replied in a fright:
He that's hang'd before noon, ought to think of to-night.
Tell your beads, quoth the priest, and be fairly truss'd up,
For you surely to-night shall in Paradise sup.
Derry down, &c.

Alas! quoth the squire, howe'er sumptuous the treat,
Parbleu, I shall have little stomach to eat:
I should therefore esteem it great favour and grace,
Would you be so kind, as to go in my place.
Derry down, &c.

That I would, quoth the father, and thank you to
boot;
But our actions, you know, with our duty must suit.
The feast, I propos'd to you, I cannot taste;
For this night, by our order, is mark'd for a fast.
Derry down, &c.

Then turning about to the hangman, he said;
Dispatch me, I prithee, this troublesome blade:
For thy cord, and my cord both equally tie;
And we live by the gold for which other men die.
Derry down, &c.

AN EPITAPH.

Stet quicunque volet potens
Aulæ culmine lubrico, &c. SENECA.

INTERR'D beneath this marble stone
Lie sauntering Jack and idle Joan.
While rolling threescore years and one
Did round this globe their courses run;
If human things went ill or well;
If changing empires rose or fell;
The morning past, the evening came,
And found this couple still the same.
They walk'd and eat, good folks: what then?
Why then they walk'd and eat again:

They soundly slept the night away;
They just did nothing all the day;
And having buried children four,
Would not take pains to try for more:
Nor sister either had, nor brother;
They seem'd just tallied for each other.
  Their moral and economy
Most perfectly they made agree:
Each virtue kept its proper bound,
Nor trespass'd on the other's ground.
Nor fame, nor censure they regarded;
They neither punish'd nor rewarded.
He car'd not what the footman did;
Her maids she neither prais'd nor chid;
So every servant took his course;
And bad at first, they all grew worse.
Slothful disorder fill'd his stable;
And sluttish plenty deck'd her table.
Their beer was strong; their wine was port;
Their meal was large; their grace was short.
They gave the poor the remnant meat,
Just when it grew not fit to eat.
  They paid the church and parish rate;
And took, but read not the receipt:
For which they claim their Sunday's due,
Of slumbering in an upper pew.
  No man's defects sought they to know;
So never made themselves a foe.
No man's good deeds did they commend;
So never rais'd themselves a friend.

Nor cherish'd they relations poor;
That might decrease their present store:
Nor barn nor house did they repair;
That might oblige their future heir.
  They neither added nor confounded;
They neither wanted nor abounded.
Each Christmas they accompts did clear,
And wound their bottom round the year.
Nor tear nor smile did they employ
At news of public grief, or joy.
When bells were rung, and bonfires made,
If ask'd, they ne'er denied their aid;
Their jug was to the ringers carried,
Whoever either died, or married.
Their billet at the fire was found,
Whoever was depos'd, or crown'd.
  Nor good, nor bad, nor fools, nor wise;
They would not learn, nor could advise:
Without love, hatred, joy, or fear,
They led—a kind of—as it were:
Nor wish'd, nor car'd, nor laugh'd, nor cried:
And so they liv'd, and so they died.

HORACE, LIB. I. EPIST. IX. IMITATED.

Septimius, Claudi, nimirum intelligit unus,
Quanti me facias, &c.

TO THE RIGHT HONOURABLE MR. HARLEY.[1]

Dear Dick,[2] howe'er it comes into his head,
Believes as firmly as he does his creed,
That you and I, Sir, are extremely great;
Though I plain Mat, you minister of state:
One word from me, without all doubt, he says,
Would fix his fortune in some little place.
Thus better than myself, it seems, he knows
How far my interest with my patron goes;
And answering all objections I can make,
Still plunges deeper in his dear mistake.
From this wild fancy, Sir, there may proceed
One wilder yet, which I foresee and dread;
That I, in fact, a real interest have,
Which to my own advantage I would save,
And, with the usual courtier's trick, intend
To serve myself, forgetful of my friend.

[1] Robert Harley, Esq. afterwards Earl of Oxford and Mortimer.

[2] This was Richard Shelton, Esq. one of the interlocutors in the poem of Alma. Mr. Prior in his will styles him his dear friend and companion.

To shun this censure, I all shame lay by,
And make my reason with his will comply;
Hoping for my excuse, 'twill be confess'd,
That of two evils I have chose the least.
So, Sir, with this epistolary scroll,
Receive the partner of my inmost soul:
Him you will find in letters, and in laws
Not unexpert, firm to his country's cause,
Warm in the glorious interest you pursue,
And, in one word, a good man and a true.

TO MR. HARLEY, WOUNDED BY GUISCARD.[1]

——————— ab ipso
Ducit opes animumque ferro. HOR.

In one great now, superior to an age,
  The full extremes of Nature's force we find:
How heavenly virtue can exalt; or rage
  Infernal, how degrade the human mind.

[1] Antoine De Guiscard had been Abbot De Borly, near the Cevennes in France, but being of a vicious and profligate disposition, he committed offences which obliged him to fly from his country. He afterwards entered into the army, and was made colonel of a regiment of horse, and lieuteuant-general, with pensions both from England and Holland. He afterwards, to make his peace with France, became a spy on the English court; was discovered, and

While the fierce monk does at his trial stand,
He chews revenge, abjuring his offence:
Guile in his tongue, and murder in his hand,
He stabs his judge to prove his innocence.

The guilty stroke and torture of the steel
Infix'd, our dauntless Briton scarce perceives:
The wounds his country from his death must feel,
The patriot views; for those alone he grieves.

The barbarous rage that durst attempt thy life,
Harley, great counsellor, extends thy fame:
And the sharp point of cruel Guiscard's knife,
In brass and marble carves thy deathless name.

Faithful assertor of thy country's cause,
Britain with tears shall bathe thy glorious wound:
She for thy safety shall enlarge her laws,
And in her statutes shall thy worth be found.

Yet midst her sighs she triumphs, on the hand
Reflecting, that diffus'd the public woe;
A stranger to her altars, and her land:
No son of hers could meditate this blow.

taken before the council to be examined, when in a fit of madness and despair he stabbed Mr. Harley with a penknife which he had secreted. He was immediately secured, but died in Newgate a few days after, of some wounds he received in the scuffle. A very particular account of this transaction by Dean Swift and Mrs. Manley is printed in the Supplement to the former's works.

Meantime thy pain is gracious Anna's care:
  Our queen, our saint, with sacrificing breath,
Softens thy anguish: in her powerful prayer
  She pleads thy service, and forbids thy death.

Great as thou art, thou canst demand no more,
  O breast bewail'd by earth, preserv'd by heaven!
No higher can aspiring virtue soar:
  Enough to thee of grief, and fame is given.

AN EXTEMPORE INVITATION TO THE EARL OF OXFORD, LORD HIGH TREASURER, MDCCXII.

MY LORD,

Our weekly friends to-morrow meet
At Matthew's palace, in Duke-street,
To try for once, if they can dine
On bacon-ham, and mutton-chine.
If wearied with the great affairs,
Which Britain trusts to Harley's cares,
Thou, humble statesman, mayst descend,
Thy mind one moment to unbend,
To see thy servant from his soul
Crown with thy health the sprightly bowl:

Among the guests, which e'er my house
Receiv'd, it never can produce
Of honour a more glorious proof—
Though Dorset us'd to bless the roof.

END OF VOL. I.

www.ingramcontent.com/pod-product-compliance
Lightning Source LLC
LaVergne TN
LVHW020216110826
845151LV00003B/736
* 9 7 8 1 4 2 5 5 3 3 9 3 9 *